EVERYTHING PARENTS SHOULD KNOW ABOUT DRUGS

SARAH LAWSON was born in London, and brought up in rural Oxfordshire. She spent five years as a postal counsellor and leaflet writer for the problem page of *Woman's Own* magazine, and now works as a freelance journalist, concentrating mainly on family issues. She is also the author of *Helping Children Cope with Bullying* (Sheldon Press, 1994). Sarah lives in Berkshire with her partner and four children.

First published in Great Britain in 1995
Sheldon Press, SPCK, Marylebone Road, London NW1 4DU

British Library Cataloguing-in-Publication Data
A catalogue record for this book is available from the British Library
ISBN 0-85969-708-8

Typesetting by Sarah Lawson, using Lotus AmiPro 3.0 software
Printed in Great Britain by Biddles Ltd, Guildford and King's Lynn

To Don, my partner and friend

Contents

Acknowledgements

Everyone wants to help reverse the rising trend in drug abuse among the young, and wherever I turned for help and information in writing this book I received unstinting support. In particular, I would like to thank Anne Marshall, Director, and Vida Guinn, Secretary, at ADFAM National for their encouragement and support, staff at Release for the pains they took in helping me sort out some complicated legal queries, ISDD's library department for tracking down exactly the information I needed, Peter and Anne Stoker of Positive Prevention Plus for sharing the fruits of their experience, and, especially, Kate Merril for her timely support and advice.

My special thanks, also, to the parents, children, and others who shared their experiences with me while I was researching this book. Although not all of their stories appear in these pages, none of the effort it cost them to talk about often very painful issues was wasted – every one of them added to my understanding of the problems of drug abuse and made an immeasurable contribution to the finished work.

1
Setting the scene

The word 'drugs' is, in itself, enough to strike terror into the hearts of most parents. Perhaps we think of a hopeless junkie, arms scarred with needle marks and abscesses, thin, dirty, unkempt, sleeping in derelict houses, thinking only of the next fix, and doomed to a premature and lonely death. There are such people, of course, but fortunately only a small proportion of illegal drug use leads to tragedies of this sort. Some of the most tragic and damaging cases of drug abuse, on the other hand, involve substances that are quite legal and easily obtainable – substances that, perhaps, we as parents should be *more* aware of and worried about than many of us are at present.

As we will see in this chapter, drugs are a real and growing problem, and one that has moved rapidly down the age scale in recent years, adding yet another concern to the long list of worries that parents already have to cope with. Like it or not, drugs are here to stay, and we need to find out all we can about this relatively new threat to our children if we are to tackle it effectively. It is vitally important that we are able to communicate with our children about drugs, and that they are able to express any problems or anxieties they may have about the subject. In order to achieve this openness, we first need to arm ourselves with a full understanding of what the problem really involves. This book aims to provide parents with that knowledge, and to dispel the vague misconceptions and half-truths that do so much to make parents feel powerless and panic-stricken whenever drugs are mentioned.

What are drugs?

Before we can begin to look at the extent of drug use among children and young people, we need to be clear just what we mean by drugs, and where we draw our personal line between responsible and irresponsible drug use. We also need to be clear about our own ambivalence towards drugs – for example, parents who roundly condemn all drugs in the strongest possible terms, but smoke 30 cigarettes a day, pour a drink before they tackle a telephone call to the boss, who depend on the support of tranquillizers to get through the day, or sleeping pills to get through the night, may find that they are sadly short of credibility in the eyes of their offspring. Children tend to have a particularly well-developed sense of fair play and honesty, so any hint of hypocrisy will immediately knock the bottom out of your argument, however well-founded it may be.

So, what is a drug? My dictionary gives two distinct definitions. First, any synthetic or natural chemical substance used in the treatment, prevention, or diagnosis of disease. Second, a chemical substance, especially a narcotic, taken for the pleasant effects it produces. Many drugs are prescribed by doctors or bought over the counter every day and used to good effect to combat disease, pain, and so on. We think of these as 'good' drugs, or perhaps don't think of them as drugs at all. There are other substances, too, that fall within the definition of drugs but are so familiar to us, and so much a part of everyone's daily life, that we don't think of them as such. Alcohol, the nicotine in tobacco, even caffeine (present in coffee, tea, and many soft drinks), fall into this category, and I have included them in the list of drugs described in Chapter 10. When we talk of 'the drug problem', however, these are not the substances that most of us have in mind. For most parents, it is the use of illegal drugs that causes the most anxiety, combined with the relatively new problem of solvent abuse (glue sniffing), which is not illegal but has been widely acknowledged as an increasing problem, almost exclusively confined to the young. There are good reasons why the use of illegal drugs should worry us so much, but the rising use of tobacco and alcohol among school-age children, and even the misuse of over-the-counter drugs such as painkillers, decongestants, and cough linctuses also needs to be addressed if we are to protect our children from the dangers that all drug use presents, both now and in their adult lives.

No one wants their child to be involved in activities that will bring them into conflict with the law, but when we talk to our children about drugs we really need to be aware of the wider issues. They need to be warned about the dangers of experimenting with substances that can lead to dependency, or that carry immediate physical dangers of use or overuse, and if we restrict our attentions to illegal drugs, we will be overlooking some of the most harmful and widely available substances that they are likely to encounter.

How big is the problem?

One of the most comprehensive sources of information about drug use in the UK is the two-yearly British Crime Survey. The 1992 Survey indicates that at least 1 in 20 adults, and probably nearer 1 in 10, have used illegal drugs at some time during their lives, and that in any one year at least 3 per cent of the adult population (approaching one and a half million people) takes an illegal drug of some sort.

Cannabis is the most widely used of the illegal drugs. Most people who have ever used an illegal drug at all have used cannabis – possibly around 5 per cent of the general population – and the majority of these have usually used it only on an occasional basis. Only around 0.33 per cent of the population have ever injected an illegal drug. Interestingly, there is a marked difference between the sexes as far as the use of illegal drugs is concerned. Roughly twice as many men as women admit to ever having used illegal drugs at all.

The use of illegal drugs peaks between the ages of 16 and 35, particularly regarding the use of cannabis, which the British Crime Survey found to be practically abandoned by those over 35 years old. A national survey conducted by Gallup for Wrangler in 1992 found that 29 per cent of the 15 to 24 year olds sampled had tried illegal drugs or solvents

3

(which are not illegal), and 23 per cent had used cannabis. Amphetamines were the next most commonly tried drug, followed by LSD (10 per cent) and ecstasy (7 per cent). 'Hard drugs', such as heroin and cocaine, had been tried by only 1 per cent of the sample. Solvent use showed strong regional variations, having been tried by 4 per cent in London and the South of England, as opposed to almost 10 per cent elsewhere.

Schoolchildren

Most surveys show that illegal drug use is much less common among children under 16 than in young adults of 16 and over. A survey carried out by John Balding of Exeter University's Schools Health Education Unit in 1991, using a large sample of pupils aged 12 -16 from 142 schools, found that 6 per cent of pupils aged 12-13 had tried illegal drugs or solvents once or more, with the numbers rising to 11 per cent at 13-14, 19 per cent at 14-15 and 22 per cent at 15-16, although the sample used was not strictly representative of the population in general. Again, cannabis and solvents were the most commonly tried drugs, followed by amphetamines, hallucinogenic (magic) mushrooms, LSD, and ecstasy, with heroin and cocaine coming at the bottom of the list. Other, smaller scale surveys have reached similar conclusions. Again, there are strong regional variations, with the rates of illegal drug use within the population of individual schools having been shown in one study to vary from 57 per cent in one area to 8 per cent in another.

Most surveys have concentrated on the numbers of young people who have used illegal drugs or solvents once or more, not those who use them frequently or regularly. Although by 15-16 years of age between a fifth and a quarter of young people will have *tried* illegal drugs or solvents, only around 2 per cent will be using cannabis on a *regular* basis, and under 1 per cent will use other drugs regularly.

What sort of child becomes involved in drug abuse?
As we can see from the statistics listed above, children in some areas and attending some schools are more likely to be offered illegal drugs than others, and boys will be statistically more willing than girls to experiment with drug use, by a ratio of perhaps 2 to 1. Regional variations, however, may not be simply a case of increased availability bringing about increased use. Social factors with a regional bias, such as unemployment, poor housing, lack of recreational facilities and the quality of life and expectations of the young population, are likely to have a strong influence on drug uptake. In short, boredom and hopelessness can make the immediate benefits of drug use attractive to youngsters, while the long-term drawbacks may not seem very important in an environment where the future doesn't have much to offer anyway.

Drug use occurs among children from all social groups and backgrounds, however, and not one of us as parents can confidently say that our child is 'not the type' to try drugs.

Children may try drugs for the following reasons:

- because they're there – the opportunity arose, and the child was curious
- because their friends were doing it and they didn't want to be left out
- because there's nothing else to do
- because someone said that they would be a wimp if they didn't
- because they were feeling unhappy or confused and looking for something to make them feel better
- because they wanted to do something risky, daring and rebellious

There is a clearer distinction, however, when it comes to the continued use of drugs, rather than just one-off use or occasional experimentation. There do seem to be some clearly identifiable factors that predispose the individual

5

child to continued drug use, although these are often recognized only after the event. They include:

- low self-esteem
- family problems
- problems at school
- lack of direction and goals
- a feeling of powerlessness

We shall look at these factors in more detail in Chapter 2.

Where are children likely to encounter and obtain drugs?
Stories appearing in the media have suggested that drug dealers are making concerted efforts to draw younger and younger children into drug use, and some have given the impression that there is a drug pusher outside every school gate, handing out free samples in the hope that they will get as many children hooked as possible. This scenario is largely fictitious. For most younger children, school is the major source of social contact with their peers, so it is inevitable that much of their knowledge and experience of drugs will come from within their school population, often from older friends. For most, their first and sometimes only, experience of illegal drugs will probably be the result of an offer at a party, or an impromptu gathering in a park, or someone's flat. For the older teenager, discos and pay-parties are a common source of drugs, notably ecstasy, LSD, and amphetamines, which are inextricably linked with the dance culture that has grown up among young people in recent years. As we have seen, the use of 'hard' drugs, like heroin and cocaine, is very rare among the young, but those who do use them will probably have been introduced to them by a friend, who may continue to supply them as a way of subsidizing their own use, or introduce them to a supplier.

Because solvents are easily available over the counter and are not illegal, users don't have to get involved in the illegal drugs scene at all in order to use them, and there is some evidence to suggest that solvent users are more likely to move on to alcohol than to the use of illegal drugs.

Another source of experience with drugs that shouldn't be overlooked is the presence of prescribed but unfinished drugs in medicine cabinets throughout the country. These may lead to experimentation by curious children, so they should be returned to a pharmacist for safe disposal.

Pocket money prices

Where schoolchildren are concerned, price will often limit the sort and amount of drugs they can try. The drugs most commonly used by the younger age group are well within the bounds of pocket money or paper round wages. Cannabis resin costs about £15 per eighth of an ounce (enough for up to ten 'joints', depending on the strength required), ecstasy around £20 per tablet, amphetamine sulphate £10 per 'wrap', and LSD as little as £2-5 per impregnated paper square. The price of 'hard' drugs is much higher. Cocaine can cost £80-100 per gramme (a regular user might get through this much in a day, although an experimental user could make it last much longer), heroin costs around £100 per gramme (with regional variations), enough for experimental use by several people, or over several days.

What happens to children who abuse drugs?

Most school-age children who use illegal drugs and solvents will do so on an experimental or occasional basis, and their use is likely to involve drugs like cannabis, ecstasy, amphetamines, and LSD. None of these drugs is without its dangers, and a few users will suffer physical or psychological damage (very rarely, this damage may prove fatal), on their first or very limited use, and a few will progress to heavier use and harder drugs, with a small proportion of these becoming addicted. Most, however, will move on from drug use altogether, or to the more socially acceptable (although still potentially dangerous) use of legal drugs, like alcohol or tobacco.

A few school-age or older teenage drug users will fall foul of the law as a result of their drug use, either because they have been caught in possession of or supplying drugs, or because their drug use has led on to other antisocial behaviour – causing a disturbance in a public place, getting into fights, vandalism, stealing, or driving under the influence of drugs, for instance. Those who are using what are considered to be the less dangerous drugs, like cannabis, are unlikely to be prosecuted for possession alone on their first offence, although supplying others will be far more likely to lead to charges and even a criminal record. The younger the child, the less likely it is that a prosecution will result, and children under ten years old cannot be prosecuted at all in the UK (eight years in Scotland). Where younger children are concerned, the authorities may decide to take them into care or to place them under a supervision order if they think that their behaviour is out of control (see Chapter 9 for more details regarding drugs and the law).

Although the drugs most likely to be used by the younger first-time or occasional user are relatively cheap, a drug habit – even involving the less expensive substances – soon becomes very expensive to maintain. Where a degree of psychological or physical dependency develops, the need to get regular supplies of drugs can become so important that it outweighs moral and social inhibitions, and the user may turn to crime to finance their habit. The proportion of drug-related crime is rising steeply, and this connection with crime is one of the less obvious dangers of drug use that may easily be overlooked by parents overwhelmed by the much-publicized *physical* dangers of some drugs.

Only a small proportion of regular drug users will, in fact, die as a result of their habit. In 1990, there were 300 deaths in the UK directly attributed to the abuse of drugs, including solvents (but not including alcohol or tobacco, which have a far worse track record in this respect) by all categories of users – dependent, regular, and occasional. Less easily quantified and more widespread, however, are the disastrous effects that drugs can have on all aspects of the user's life and their family's. There are no statistics to show how many relationships have ended, jobs have been lost, exams failed and opportunities wasted, how much unhappiness has been caused, and how many crimes committed as a direct or indirect result of drug use. The use of drugs at an early age can slow or stop the difficult business of progressing towards emotional maturity, leaving the user without the internal resources to cope with life without the support of drugs. Even if we feel, as parents, that the risk to our children of physical or psychological damage as a result of drug abuse is small, this greater risk – that of damage to the quality of life of our children and all who care for them – should concern us all.

2
Substances and effects

Commonly misused substances can be listed under broad categories according to their effects on the user. There are problems with any system of classification, however: the effects of some drugs cross two or more categories, and some have differing effects depending on the dose taken, and even the setting in which they are used. The classifications used here, therefore, are intended to serve as a rough guide to the likely effect of the drug, and should not be taken to be definitive.

Depressants (downers)
This group includes tranquillizing drugs, like benzodiazepines and barbiturates, which are prescribed by doctors to relieve anxiety and aid sleep, as well as alcohol, and solvents. All these drugs work by depressing the central nervous system, calming the user down, and, ultimately, causing loss of consciousness.

Stimulants (uppers)
These include amphetamines, cocaine and tobacco. In low doses, stimulants relieve fatigue and aid concentration. Higher doses can produce a feeling of exhilaration and power, increased energy and ability to concentrate, confidence and the ability to go without sleep or food for long periods. Physical effects can include a rise in blood pressure, increased breathing and heart rate, widening of the pupils, dryness of the mouth, diarrhoea, and increased urination.

Opiates
Opiates have a depressant and calming effect on the user. Unlike the downers mentioned above, though, they also

produce a feeling of euphoria. Opiate users often say that the drug makes them feel as though they are 'wrapped in cotton wool', and this makes opiates particularly attractive to those who are struggling with emotional problems they feel unable to cope with.

Hallucinogens

Hallucinogens, such as LSD, cause intensification and distortion of sensory experiences, such as colour, sound and touch. Depending on the dose taken, the user may 'see' sounds and 'hear' colours, his surroundings may seem to shift and change, and his sense of time may be distorted. Cannabis is technically a very mild hallucinogen, and ecstasy (MDMA) is a combined hallucinogen and stimulant.

Anabolic steroids

Anabolic steroid drugs are a synthetic version of hormones that occur naturally in the body. They are used by bodybuilders and athletes to build up muscle, but can cause aggressive behaviour and severe, irreversible damage to the body when taken for long periods and in non-medicinal doses.

Over-the-counter drugs

Some preparations that can be bought without a prescription contain small quantities of controlled drugs. Others are free of controls, but may be misused for their side-effects. Antihistamines can cause drowsiness, for instance, and are sometimes used in conjunction with other drugs to heighten or offset their effects. Laxatives may be misused by girls suffering from eating disorders. Using these drugs in doses far higher than were intended can have unpredictable and dangerous effects, so the fact that they are freely available is no guarantee that they will not cause harm.

Others

Some substances, such as amyl and butyl nitrites, which cause blood vessels to dilate, do not fit into any of the above categories. In their quest for a new 'high', some drug users will experiment with almost any substance – even those that were never intended for use on the human body – and new drugs and combinations of drugs are constantly being developed by unscrupulous entrepeneurs, often finding their way through loopholes in the drug laws in the process.

It is impossible to list here all the substances that have been or could be abused, but those in common use and most easily available are listed in detail in Chapter 10, along with the dangers specific to each. Some dangers, however, relate to the method or circumstances of manufacture, supply, and administration rather than to the drug itself. Injecting is particularly dangerous in this respect. The general risks of drug taking include the following.

- *Overdose*

The user may take too much in one go, which can have unexpected or damaging results.

- *Overuse*

The user may indulge in use of the drug to the point where his ability to carry on a normal life is affected and may fail to develop or lose the ability to cope with life in other ways; some users will become addicted to some drugs.

- *Accident*

Most drugs affect coordination and reaction time, so that accidents when driving or operating machinery, falls, and so on become more likely.

- *Adulteration*

Illicit drugs are not subject to the same controls as legitimate products, so may be impure or of unknown strength. The adulterant may be harmful in itself (it has been known for strychnine or rat poison to be used for this purpose). On the other hand, a fatal overdose can occur where the drug is mixed with *less* adulterant than usual; the dose the user habitually takes will contain more of the drug than she expects.

- *Mixing drugs*
Taking more than one drug at a time, or even within several hours of each other, can change and increase their effects and the likelihood that they will do harm.

- *Deterioration in lifestyle*
Habitual drug users may neglect their health, or spend so much money on drugs that they cannot afford to feed or house themselves properly.

- *Involvement in criminal activity*
Possessing and dealing in many drugs is a criminal offence. Heavy users may finance their habit by turning to crime or prostitution.

- *Dangers arising from injection*
Whatever the drug used, injection introduces its own risks. The danger of an overdose is increased; infection can occur as a result of the use of non-sterile equipment, with serious diseases, such as hepatitis and AIDS, becoming a real risk where needles and syringes are shared. Poor injection technique and the injection of substances that are not prepared for that purpose, such as crushed tablets, can cause abscesses, gangrene and other serious health problems.

Dependence and addiction

Not all children who have the opportunity to become involved in drug use will do so. Of those who do experiment, only a small proportion will go on to use drugs regularly, and a few of these will develop a degree of psychological dependency or full-blown psychological and physical addiction. Why? What makes one child more susceptible to the effects of drugs than another, and what can we do to influence these factors in our children?

Although there is no easily identifiable drug-taking 'type', professionals working with drug users have identified certain factors that crop up again and again in the people they work with, and which they believe make young people more likely to become reliant on drugs.

- *Low self-esteem and lack of confidence*
For those who feel inadequate and unsure of themselves, drugs can offer a feeling of new confidence and an escape from their anxieties about themselves. These feelings can open up new possibilities for making friends and taking part in activities, and are a powerful stimulus to keep using them.

- *Feelings of powerlessness*
Youngsters who feel trapped in a dead-end existence that they are powerless to influence or change, or at the mercy of feelings that they can't control or live with, may be attracted by the measure of control over their feelings, albeit temporary, that drugs can offer. They know that, at least for as long as the drug lasts, they will feel a certain way – euphoric, relaxed, confident, and so on.

- *Unhappiness at home, perhaps because of abuse, neglect, or family break-ups*
Drugs can offer a brief escape from unhappiness, perhaps the only escape for the child who feels unable to turn to family and friends for support or talk to anyone about his worries.

- *The 'wild child' syndrome*
There are some children who simply seem to need more excitement and stimulation than others, who need to take risks and find ever more challenging experiences. Where their needs have not been channelled into safer areas, these

children may be irresistibly attracted by the new and unpredictable experiences offered by some drugs, while being unconcerned or even encouraged by the dangers.

• *Physical susceptibility to the effects of drugs*
Some people seem to be physically more susceptible to the effects of drugs than others. They may be affected more profoundly, become dependent more quickly and have more difficulty in stopping drug use than other, less susceptible people, even in the absence of any particular emotional problems.

What is dependence?

We say that someone has become dependent on a drug when, usually after repeated use but occasionally after only limited experience, they feel an overriding need to use the substance on a regular basis. Broadly speaking, dependence is divided into two categories, but, often, both aspects are present and it is often very difficult for the user to distinguish between the two.

• *Psychological dependence*
Someone who uses a drug regularly may come to rely on its effects – stimulation, sedation, or a variety of other sensations – to help her escape from problems, relax, socialize, study, or just make life bearable. She may lose her ability to achieve these things in other ways, and the prospect of being without the substance makes her anxious and depressed, sometimes very severely and to the point of real mental disorder.

• *Physical dependence*
Taking drugs regularly over a long period can change the way that the body works so that, if the drug is withdrawn suddenly, it cannot function normally. This can result in a variety of very unpleasant physical symptoms, such as nausea and vomiting, sweating, cramps, tremors,

sleeplessness, and   convulsions, which, after withdrawal from very heavy use of some drugs, can prove fatal.

The situation is further complicated by the development of tolerance of some drugs after repeated use. Although it is not the case with all drugs, the body can build up a resistance to some so that their effect is reduced, and the user will need to take higher and higher doses to achieve the same result. Regular users may, without ill-effect, take doses that would cause illness or even death in a first-time user. Problems sometimes arise when a regular user, after a period without the drug, takes the dose he was accustomed to taking before he stopped. Because his body's tolerance of the substance has diminished, he may become very ill as a result.

What is addiction?

The word 'addiction' is often used to describe an individual's established dependence on a drug, and implies that there are damaging social, psychological, and/or physical consequences for her as a result. Most drug addiction involves both psychological and physical dependence in varying proportions, and both must be overcome if the dependent individual is successfully to escape her addiction.

We live in a society where powerful and potentially dangerous substances are all around us, and we can't turn back the clock. We have to accept that, however strict our drug laws and however stringently they are enforced, there will always be potential for young people to become involved in drug abuse. As we cannot eliminate the problem, we must give our children the means to protect themselves. In the following chapters, we look at ways of doing just that.

3

Talking to your child about drugs

There are many ways in which you, as a parent, can help your child to avoid being drawn into regular drug use. She will be best able to cope with this and any other situation where she is under pressure to take risks in order to conform or gain peer approval if she feels good about herself, that she is a worthwhile person in her own right, and deserves to be taken care of, and that what she feels and believes is important and worth sticking up for. These feelings don't arise overnight or in relation to just one issue, they need to be encouraged from early childhood (we will look at ways in which you can help your child to develop them in Chapter 4). She also needs to develop the inner resources and confidence to cope with the problems and disappointments that will inevitably arise in her life, particularly during the stormy adolescent years. If she feels powerless to change her life or influence what happens to her for the better, drugs may look like the only available escape from an intolerable situation. Again, the confidence and self-knowledge that get us through crises are not acquired quickly, they are built up over the years as we tackle and overcome, first, the small traumas of baby and toddlerhood, and then the bigger challenges of acquiring independence, going to school, making and maintaining friendships, and, ultimately, leaving home.

Building these strengths is a long-term job, although it is never too late to start and a little thought and effort on your part can make your family environment a positive resource for your child, in this and many other respects. There is, however, one thing that every parent can do, and do now – whatever the age of their child and whether or not he has already been exposed to drugs and drug use – and that is to ensure that he has full and accurate information about the drugs he may encounter, their effects on the body and mind, and the dangers attached to their use. You may not feel confident at first about tackling this subject with your child, and it is true that there are sources of information about drugs outside the family for children and young people, but can you rely on these to give him all the information he needs, and will the message he receives about the misuse of drugs match your family's values and the principles against which your child has been brought up to measure his standards and behaviour? It is unlikely that they will. The approach taken will almost certainly be dictated by a variety of factors, not all of them embodying the best interests of the individual child.

Where will your child learn about drugs?

The following are the most common and easily accessible sources of information about drugs, and your child will almost certainly come into contact with most or all of them at one time or another.

School
The general subject of drugs is part of the National Science Curriculum from primary age upwards. At its simplest level, the infant teacher may explain to the five year olds in her class that medicines may *look* like sweets, but that they can be dangerous. She may point out that the bottle of pills the doctor or chemist gave mummy will be safe for her to take, as long as she takes only the amount it says on the bottle or packet, but that no one else should take them.

When it comes to illegal drugs, like cannabis or heroin, or potentially dangerous but legal ones, like alcohol, the approach taken by different schools varies widely. National Curriculum requirements are not specific, and timetabling is up to the school. The subject of drug use may be covered in science lessons, tutorials, lifeskills, personal and social education, or humanities, for instance, and the approach will vary according to the time available, the views and priorities of the headteacher, staff, governors, and the individual teacher leading the session, as well as pressure from parents (some of whom may not want their children given information they feel will make drug use more likely or easier).

If you intend to rely on the school to provide your child with the information he needs when making decisions about drugs, it would be wise to find out from the school exactly how and when the subject will be covered. Ask specifically whether the school will be delivering an antidrugs message or whether they will stick to an account of the drugs that children may encounter, their effects, and methods of use.

Even if you feel that the school can and will provide your child with all the factual information she needs, it is still important that she is able to talk to you, her parents, about any concerns she may have regarding drugs and drug use. It is important that you are well informed and that the subject is open for discussion in your family. Ideally, this openness needs to be established long before any worries or problems arise. Increasingly, local authority drugs and health advisers are organizing sessions for parents in schools, in which full information on the drugs available to children, the scale of use in the area, and the ways in which children can be helped and protected are made available in an informal way. These can be an invaluable source of information and reassurance, and are well worth attending if they take place in your area.

Friends
Much of what children hear about drugs is likely to come from their peers. Most of this will probably relate to the availability and prices of drugs locally, or consist of the accounts – possibly second- or third-hand – of what using a particular drug feels like. Children may pick up some useful information this way, but it won't give them an accurate or complete picture of the effects on the body or the addictive qualities and possible risks of each substance, and is likely to be coloured by the wish of the storyteller to appear knowledgeable and streetwise.

Media

For many children and parents, accounts in the media are the main source of information about drugs. Unfortunately, the information given is often inaccurate and may be misleading. When a public figure dies in circumstances that might possibly be drug-related, there is a sudden storm of headlines about 'the drug menace', junkies, and the spectre of the drug pusher at the school gate. The reports under these headlines tend to be long on sensationalism and short on accurate information, and often serve to feed both the panic reaction of parents and the perception by adolescents of drug-taking as a glamorous activity, taken part in by exciting and creative people who live hard and die young. Again, they often serve to distort the picture and are not helpful to young people making decisions about their own lives. Television documentaries, while they often present a reasonably balanced and informed view of a particular aspect of drug use, cannot cover the whole issue. On their own, they are not enough to ensure that your child understands the issues involved.

Youth clubs and voluntary youth groups

Youth group leaders may decide to encourage drugs awareness among their members by making information available, leading group discussions, or by more formal means, although they are not obliged to do so and many may not feel equipped to tackle the subject anyway. Again, it is important that you know what information your child is receiving, and your child's group leader should be able and willing to tell you whether and how the subject is being covered.

What have parents got to offer?

As we can see, your child may already have absorbed a good deal of information about drugs from a variety of sources, but this information may be unbalanced. Even if he has been presented with a good, factual account of drug misuse, perhaps in a personal and social education lesson or a session at a youth club, he is unlikely to absorb all that he needs to know in one session – there will be occasions when he wants to clarify something he has heard at school or reassure himself about an experience he has had and, although he might be able to get the information or support he needs from a teacher or youth worker, they are not as easily available as you, and can't have the same loving concern for or understanding of your child that you have.

Your child cannot and should not make important decisions about her life in an emotional vacuum. Only you can talk to and, equally importantly, listen to your child about drugs within the framework of family life and from the standpoint of someone who cares about her and her future. She needs the facts, but she also needs your input to help her interpret the impact of those facts on her life and the lives and expectations of the whole family. What you think and feel as a parent is important to your child, even though she may be reluctant to admit it even to herself, and your attitudes and opinions will influence the way she feels and the decisions she makes. She needs to know what you feel, as well as what you know about the problem, although you both need to be clear where facts end and feelings begin.

The facts about drugs are easy to learn, and this book should give you all the information you will need to talk to your child about the drugs he may encounter, the effects they can have, and the dangers they can present. (If you or your child want to know more, you can refer to the useful addresses and further reading sections, pages 123-128 for sources of more detailed information).

The feelings can be more difficult to handle, and it is important that you think through your feelings about the possibility of your child using drugs before you launch into a major discussion of the problem. Otherwise, you may be taken by surprise by the strength of your own reactions to your child's opinions on the subject, and constructive discussion could be difficult.

How do I do it?

You have decided that you want to talk to your child about drugs, but how do you go about it? Should you corner him in his bedroom and launch into a lecture, approach it casually over supper, or wait for him to bring the subject up himself? With luck, the subject will come up in conversation as the result of something you or your child see on television or the papers. Perhaps your child will tell you about an incident from his own or a friend's experience – he may know someone who is using drugs, or have been offered them at a party. If it doesn't, however, how about asking his opinion on a drug-related issue, rather than launching into a lecture. Ask 'Do you think that many people at your school have used drugs?', 'Why do you think that more young people are using drugs these days?' However the subject comes up, try to remember the following three key points.

- *Don't panic*

Even if your worst nightmares come true, and she tells you that she has taken or is taking drugs, don't give in to your understandable urge to shout about how stupid she has been, lock her in her bedroom and find, and dismember, the person who supplied her with the substance. The fact that you and your child are talking together about drugs is good. While your feelings are quite natural, giving in to them could effectively close the open channel of communication between yourself and your child, and make it impossible for you to give her the support she needs, now and in the future. She may be very frightened herself, although she may try to cover this up with bravado and apparent unconcern or defiance, and need you to be strong for her, and help her find the confidence she needs to get the situation under control.

- *Be honest*

It may be tempting to overstate the case against drug use to your child, in the hope that he will be so frightened of the consequences that he never dares to experiment. This rarely works. Whatever you tell him about the dangers of drug use, he will hear accounts from friends, and may even have had experiences himself, that tell him that drugs do not always lead to disaster. You will help him more by telling the truth, and he will know that he can trust you for honest advice and support if he ever gets into a situation that he is worried about.

This doesn't mean that you should reel off the facts dispassionately. You do, after all, love and care about her. It would be surprising if you *didn't* have opinions and worries about drug use, and it is fine to tell her about these. Your caring about her and what she does is important to her own self-image. If you don't care about her taking risks, why should she? By all means tell her how worried and upset you would be if she took drugs, but don't expect this alone to make the difference between her experimenting and not.

- *Be realistic*
Adolescence is a time for establishing independence from your parents and all that they stand for, and for finding out what sort of person you are in your own right. One of the ways in which children have always done this is by taking part in activities they know their parents would disapprove of and often (especially where boys are concerned) that carry some risk. We have all seen the boy riding to school with his cycle helmet hanging on his handlebars, and we know that he took it off as soon as he was out of sight of home. Everyone has heard stories of girls who have gone to forbidden discos on the pretext of staying with friends. Experimenting with drugs has all the elements to appeal to the adolescent at this stage in his development, and we as parents have to accept, however much we wish that it were not so, that our children may dabble with drugs whatever we say. Armed with accurate information and the feeling that they are worth protecting, however, they will be more likely to pass through this phase without doing anything that will have irreversible consequences on their physical, mental or emotional health. It

is realistic for parents to aim to provide them with these, but not to expect that they can prevent drugs from entering their lives at all, although this is what we would all prefer. Keeping from our children the knowledge that could make drug use safer is not a wise option.

How do I deal with awkward questions?
- *Did you ever try drugs?*

Well, did you? Most of us who have teenage children today grew up in a social environment where drug use was almost the norm, and drugs of many kinds have been in use throughout the lifetime of everyone who has become a parent since. If you did experiment briefly with drugs yourself, you may gain your child's respect by saying so, and by telling her why you didn't carry your experimentation any further. If you have had a real problem with drugs – even those like alcohol or tobacco, which are legal and socially acceptable – telling your child first hand how badly your life and relationships can be affected, and how hard it can be to stop, may make more of an impact than any number of statistics or scare stories. It can be very hard to admit to your child that you have made mistakes, especially if you have subscribed to the 'do as I say and not as I do' or 'because I know best' school of parenting. Parents don't have to be perfect, however, and seeing your parents admitting to and coping with their own mistakes can be a valuable lesson in dealing with your own.

- *Why is alcohol/smoking all right and cannabis isn't?*

If you use alcohol or tobacco on a regular basis yourself, you may find it a bit difficult to answer this one. In fact, very few people would claim that drinking and smoking are without dangers – they just happen, for historical and financial reasons, to be legal. Cannabis isn't, and this presents problems of its own that have to be taken into account along with the dangers of using any recreational drug, whether legal or not. Again, if you are a smoker or a drinker, you can tell your child first hand just how difficult it is to stop using these substances once you have started, and how important it is to use them responsibly if you do.

- *You're always telling me what to do*
Most adolescents feel like this, whether the feeling is justified or not. Sometimes parents *do* tell children what to do – 'Tidy your room', 'Hang up your coat', 'Turn the stereo down', and so on. Talking about an issue like drugs, though, is different (or should be). Explain that you want to help him equip himself to make his own decisions in life, not to make all his decisions for him. This will be easier if he has been allowed to take over some of the responsibility for his actions gradually throughout his childhood.

- *If I want to take drugs, you can't stop me*
This is true enough, but you obviously don't want your child to take chances with her life because you love and feel responsible for her, and this is as it should be. This is an issue of love and concern for your child, not one of discipline and rebellion, and it is important to keep the discussion on this level.

- *My friend took ecstasy and it didn't do him any harm*
Many people take drugs occasionally, even regularly, and come to no harm. There is no way of knowing in advance, however, whether any given individual will be one of the lucky ones or one of the few who suffer permanent damage or even death as a result of drug misuse. Because illicit drugs are often adulterated and the dose is uncertain, and because different people react in different ways even to a *known* dose of some substances, one or more safe experiences do not mean that problems will never arise, either with a new or familiar drug. Anyone taking these substances is giving away their control over what happens to their body and mind, and it is worth anyone who is considering taking drugs thinking

about whether this is something that they really want to do, whatever the short-term benefits.

The way in which you talk to your child about drugs is important, but it is not the whole story. Much of what he knows and feels about drugs and drug use is acquired in much more subtle ways, and his attitudes to the principles of drug use will probably have been formed long before you or anyone else even thinks about broaching the subject with him directly. From the earliest years, you can set an example to your child about the proper and responsible use of drugs, and help him to develop the confidence and ability to take control of and responsibility for what he does with his life. In the next chapter, we look at practical ways of encouraging both.

4

Examples and independence

Setting examples

Whatever you say to your child, ultimately the biggest influence you have on her attitudes will be through the examples you set within the family as she grows up. Attitudes to drug use are no exception.

Some of the factors that influence the way children feel about drugs are straightforward and obvious. Drugs are a part of all our lives, and the way we use them on a day-to-day basis is important in showing children that they have their place, but should not be relied on to solve all our problems:

- if you or a member of the family have to take drugs for some reason, explain why you need them, what they do, and tell them what the side-effects and dangers of that drug might be – migraine tablets help with the headache, but make you feel dopey, for instance, or your iron tablets can help you to stay healthy while you are pregnant, but could poison a child who swallowed just a few of them

- if you like the occasional drink, explain that you enjoy a glass of wine or a pint or two of beer as part of an evening out with friends, or when you are hot and thirsty from mowing the lawn, but that you are very careful not to drink so much that you feel drunk and out of control, and that you always avoid driving when you have been drinking

- make sure that drugs are treated with respect in your home. Dispose of any leftover medicines by returning them to a pharmacist, and keep any alcohol and cigarettes safely out of the reach of children

Coping

Perhaps less obviously, the way that you handle your own stresses, strains, and problems can influence the likelihood of your child using drugs. One of the factors that attracts young people to drug use, and keeps them coming back for more, is the instant relief from stress, anxiety, and doubts that it can provide. From babyhood, a large part of growing up involves developing the inner resources to cope with our own problems and worries; some will find this more difficult than others, due not only to individual and genetic differences in temperament and outlook, but also, and in large measure, to family influences. You can help your children to learn ways of coping with stress, and so reduce the likelihood that they will find something in drugs that fulfils a need they can't fulfil from their own resources. As example is so important, we need first to look at our own ways of facing stress and conflict. How do *you* cope?

- bottle it up?
- blame someone else?
- have a drink/cigarette?
- get depressed?
- avoid situations that might be upsetting?

From the child's point of view, feelings must be very dangerous things indeed if even parents can't cope with them, and the only safe thing to do must be to try to make them go away. Of course, they won't go away, and so begins a chain of events that can lead to all sorts of psychological and physical problems as the child struggles to cope with dangerous and powerful forces from which she can't escape. Drugs may form a part of her coping mechanism. How, then, can we cope with conflict constructively within the family, and equip our children to live with and acknowledge both their pleasant and their unpleasant emotions without fear?

28

The 'take a pill' mentality – developing other ways of coping

Beware of giving the impression that there is an answer to every problem and discomfort in life. Sometimes life *is* uncomfortable, physically and emotionally, but while this discomfort can be unpleasant, it is not life-threatening and often passes quickly. The remedy sought may, in fact, cause worse problems than the discomfort it is employed to tackle. In the family, this starts with simple things like taking a tablet every time you have a headache, making a fuss over every little bump and scrape and, later, trying to sort out all your children's quarrels, and protect them from every upset and disappointment. When the family pet dies, for instance, it may avoid any immediate unpleasantness to say that it has simply escaped and gone to live in the country, where it will be much happier, but this approach will deny the child the chance to experience grief and learn the valuable lesson that it passes, and that life goes on. Children need to learn that unpleasant feelings will not harm them, and will pass. Some of those who don't learn this will seek to escape or control them through the use of drugs.

You can help your child best in these emotionally difficult situations by offering support and comfort in a matter-of-fact way. Don't devalue her feelings by denying them – 'don't be silly, there's nothing to be sad about' – or lend them more importance than they merit – 'Oh God, it's awful isn't it darling. Let's go out and buy that bicycle you wanted to make you feel better'. Let her experience them in her own way and offer reassurance and a cuddle if it's wanted.

Facing up to it – conflict and confidence

There are times for every parent when family life seems to be made up almost entirely of conflict. Your children argue constantly among themselves, tease, shout, and sulk, you argue with them, and with each other about them – all very unlike the image of the happy family that we see in advertisements for breakfast cereal and soap powder. We shouldn't be misled, however, into thinking that this means there is something wrong with our children or the way we have brought them up. Families are supposed to be like this.

It is within the safety of the family that we learn to deal with disappointment, frustration, and conflict, and with the powerful feelings they raise in all of us. We all feel angry from time to time, and hurt, and jealous, and these feelings are, at first, very frightening and overwhelming – just look at the toddler having a tantrum, completely out of control and almost 'possessed' by his anger. Make no mistake about it, this is a very frightening experience for the child – he wants to destroy everything around him, and, for all he knows, may be capable of doing just that. If his caretaker stays calm, restrains him from doing damage to himself and others, and comforts and reassures him when the tantrum passes, he will soon learn that his anger is not as dangerous as he thought – he has not destroyed anything and the people he loves are still there and still love him. With this knowledge will come the beginnings of control, although it will take many years of similar experiences for him to reach emotional maturity. If, however, his caretaker loses her temper, hits him, tells him what a bad boy he is, or reacts in some other way that confirms his worst fears that his feelings are uncontrollable and dangerous, he may never feel able to cope with these dangerous feelings, and will resort to denying , suppressing or simply being taken over by them.

The same principle applies throughout childhood. As parents, we don't have to tolerate bad behaviour, but coping with children's anger and frustration by telling them that they are bad people to feel that way, or making them feel that negative emotions should be hidden and suppressed, will deny them the opportunity to find effective ways of dealing with them. Anne's parents made this kind of mistake.

There were three children in my family – I was in the middle. My mother's great wish was that we should have what she saw as a 'nice' family life together, and that meant that we should all love each other and be happy all the time. Arguments shocked and upset her, and she constantly told us that we should all be friends and be nice to one another. She and my father always treated us children with scrupulous fairness – if she spent £5 on a present for one of us, she would spend exactly the same on the others; if one of us got some sort of special attention – an outing or even just a cuddle – everyone else had to have the same.

I think she really felt this should mean that none of us should ever have anything to complain about, or ask for, but of course it didn't. We were all different, and I, for some reason, seemed to need more reassurance than my brother and sister. There were times when I felt low or anxious about something and needed a hug or just some attention, but I didn't get it – my mother just said that I should stop being silly, I was a lucky girl and had nothing to worry about. My brother and sister were happy enough most of the time, as far as my parents were concerned, so why shouldn't I be?

They felt that I was unreasonably demanding, and any expression of anger or resentment was looked on with absolute horror. They gave the clear impression that there was something wrong with me for feeling like this, and I grew up thinking that feelings of anger and hurt should always be suppressed. Of course, I couldn't make them go away, but when I was about 16 I did find something that helped – alcohol. After a few drinks, nothing seemed to matter so much any more, and I could relax with my friends and just be myself. I looked older than I was, and had no problems getting served in bars and off-licences.

For a few years, I drank really heavily, and I did quite a few things while I was drunk that I would rather forget. I really depended on alcohol for a while, and I think that I could easily have got permanently hooked. Fortunately, I met my current boyfriend, and I gradually became sure enough about his feelings for me to be able to be myself

31

with him. I've lost my temper with him once or twice, we have the occasional argument, and he hasn't stopped loving me – I can't tell you what a relief that's been – and I don't need to get drunk to hide from my feelings any more.

In every aspect of family life, your example can help or hinder your child in learning to cope constructively with difficult situations and emotions, but here are a few basic principles that you can apply in all your dealings with your child:

- *Talk about feelings – yours and hers*
  - Your child will learn from you the vocabulary that she needs to describe her feelings
  - Talking about her feelings will help her to understand and cope with them
  - Children sometimes need reassurance that the way they feel is normal

- *Accept the way he says he feels*
If you don't, he will eventually stop telling you about his feelings altogether. This may sound obvious, but how often have you heard, or taken part in, this sort of exchange:

son: I hate that school, I don't want to go there any more.
mother: Nonsense – you've always loved it there!

A more helpful response might be, 'You sound unhappy. What's happened to make you feel like this?'

- *Be positive*
It is not enough simply to tell children where they have gone wrong. Try at least to balance your criticism of your child with praise for what she gets right, and her confidence in herself will benefit immeasurably. Even where children have behaved very badly, as they sometimes do, it is important

they know that we still love them, even though we hate what they have done.

- *Expect the best*
In some families, the children are always presumed guilty until proven innocent. Adults often need someone to blame for everything that goes wrong, goes missing, or just doesn't work out as they had hoped – after all, if they don't blame someone else quickly, they may have to take the blame themselves. Faced with low expectations, children will often live down to them – why bother to try when you know that everyone will think the worst of you whatever you do? Getting the best out of your child means giving him every opportunity to do the right thing, respecting him enough to believe that he will do it most of the time and telling him how pleased and proud you are when he does. If you can do this, he will live up to your expectations – most of the time.

Confidence and peer pressure

As every parent will know, few things worry a child more than feeling different from everyone else. Just having a different style of shoe from everyone else in the class can be a major source of anxiety for many children, and having parents who are even slightly odd in a child's eyes can cause terminal embarrassment. The pressure to conform is so strong that some children will do things that they feel are wrong and take risks that worry them just to gain acceptance from their peers. When it comes to drug-taking, this peer pressure can prove a significant factor in children's decisions to participate or opt out.

The pressure to conform or impress will be greatest for children who feel uncertain about their worth or acceptability as people in their own right, and, unfortunately, a lack of self-confidence is often obvious to others and makes it more likely that they will be rejected or manipulated by other children. You can help your child to build self-confidence while she is growing up, first and most importantly by giving her your own unconditional love and acceptance, but also by:

- allowing her to become independent in her own time (see below)
- allowing her to think for herself and make decisions
- listening to and respecting her views and opinions, even if you don't always agree with them
- finding activities through which she can gain a sense of achievement and self-worth

Becoming independent

Children naturally grow towards independence, and you can help best by offering him the security he needs without smothering his independent urges. Contrary to the beliefs of many, you can't *make* a child independent. Forcing him towards too much independence too soon by, for instance, denying him the security of his mother's presence when he needs it or sending him to playgroup or nursery school before he is ready, will actually delay the day when he feels confident and able to cope on his own. Throughout childhood, however, it is important to offer new challenges and to help him over the natural doubts and insecurities he feels in taking them on. Striking this balance is one of the most difficult things a parent has to do, but it is essential if he is to build the self-confidence he needs to look after himself.

Practical ways of keeping your child out of danger

Although most children will be exposed to the availability and use of drugs, either through school contacts or others, you can protect them from this exposure to some extent by making sure that their time is filled with constructive activities in a safe environment. By the time that they are teenagers, any sudden interest in who they mix with and what they do will probably be viewed with some suspicion, so it is important to establish your input into their social and recreational lives as early as possible. The following measures will help.

• *Get to know their friends*
As we have seen, your child's friends are an important influence on her life. Make a point of getting to know them, and their parents, right from the start. You can help your child to feel confident about making friends by providing in your home a happy, safe environment in which friendships can be established. It may be bribery, but children are influenced in their choice of friends by the prospect of being shown a good time, and other parents will encourage their children to make and stay friends with yours if they know and trust you.

• *Keep them busy*
Find activities in which they can take part safely, make it possible for them to get there, and encourage them to persevere and get the most out of them. It's often a relief when your child says that she doesn't want to go to dancing classes any more – no more rushing about from place to place after school, no more expensive outfits or ballet shoes – but boredom is a significant factor in the uptake of drugs by some children. It is important that children have ongoing activities and interests that give them something constructive to do with their time, and provide them with a sense of achievement and confidence.

• *Keep open house*
When children reach the stage where they enjoy hanging around together in groups, they will need somewhere to go. It may not be everyone's idea of fun to have a bunch of hungry adolescents taking over their kitchen and giggling at incomprehensible 'in' jokes, but if they are in your house they are not hanging about on street corners or in other undesirable places. Encouraging your child and his friends to

use your home as a centre for social activities can pay off in the long run.

- *Establish limits*

Your child needs to know, right from the start, that it is important for you to know where she is, who she is with, and when she can be expected back. In an area where most of the places that your child will want to go to are some distance away, she will have to arrange transport, and providing this, perhaps in cooperation with other parents, will give you some control over the situation.

- *Give them a lifeline*

You can't reasonably expect your adolescent to stay at home every evening when her friends are going to parties or discos. You can, however, make sure that she always has a way out of any situation in which she feels uncomfortable. Tell her that you will come and pick her up without question if she gives you a ring, and that you will back up any excuse she may feel the need to make – she has to be home early because you are going out, you are ill and don't want to stay up late waiting for her, or whatever. My own teenage children are at an age where friends sometimes ring and ask them out to places they don't want to go to, or with people they don't want to be with. They sometimes feel that they need an excuse not to go, and will tell their friends that they have to check with me first. I am quite happy to play the villain of the piece, and 'forbid' them to go on some pretext or other – needing them to baby-sit or insisting that they finish their homework – and it gets them out of an embarrassing situation without losing face.

Good parenting

Parenting is a skill like any other, and it takes time to learn what works and what doesn't. In this chapter, I have tried to show in this chapter just how important parenting skills can be in the development of every child's confidence, self-esteem, and independence, but there isn't room here to do more than scratch the surface. There are, however, many good books available on various aspects of parenting, and several groups that organize parenting workshops (see pages 123-128 for further details).

5

Is my child using drugs?

What are the effects, what should I look for?

While the effects of occasional, experimental use of drugs may be short term and very hard to detect, regular use will result in changes in behaviour and physical symptoms that will be obvious to most parents. The trouble is that many of these changes could also be the result of the physical and mental upheavals of adolescence, so it can be very difficult to say with any certainty that your child is using drugs without some other corroborating evidence. The following emotional and behavioural signs, therefore, might indicate that your child is using drugs, but could also mean that he is having a struggle with the pressures of growing up:

- sudden, regular and marked mood swings
- uncharacteristic aggression
- withdrawal from activities that have previously been important to him - SEXIST
- changes in eating patterns, particularly loss of appetite
- lethargy and sleepiness, spending long periods in bed

Most parents of teenage children, however, will recognize some or all of the above as applying to their child at one time or another and in varying degrees. Although they may well worry and irritate you, it would be a mistake to be too quick to attribute them to a major or specific problem like drug abuse – adolescents are often awkward, surly, and a general pain in the neck. However, if these changes are compounded by some of the more concrete signs listed below, you may be justified in suspecting that drug use is involved:

- sudden shortage of money, with no obvious signs of where it is going

- disappearance of money or valuables belonging to other family members
- evidence of lying, secrecy, obvious attempts to cover up activities
- signs of intoxication
- unusual stains or smells on clothing
- unusual purchases or disappearance of hair spray, lighter fuel and other solvents
- sores around the mouth or nose
- plastic bags containing traces of glue
- remnants of home-made cigarettes, cigarette papers and loose tobacco
- small pieces of scorched tin foil
- small wraps of paper
- home-made pipe, possibly constructed from an empty drink can or bottle and some form of tubing.

As we saw in Chapter 1, injecting is very rare in this age group, and among the population at large. The following signs, however, may make you suspect that your child is injecting drugs:

- needle marks on the body, particularly arms and legs – a reluctance to wear clothes that might reveal these
- injecting equipment – needles, syringes, makeshift tourniquet (possibly a belt, string, or pyjama cord)
- blood stains on clothes, bedding and carpet.

Natasha's story
Natasha, 15, had always been an energetic, happy child, so her mother was worried when she started to look paler than usual, and seemed tired and listless. At first, she put it down to the stress of her forthcoming exams – Natasha was not particularly academic, and had always felt that she had to work harder than most of her friends just to achieve the same grades. She tried to get Natasha to take a break from study occasionally, but Natasha would always

say that she didn't have time for anything other than studying, and spent a lot of time at her friends' houses, apparently doing schoolwork.

Natasha's health continued to deteriorate. She always seemed tired and, although she was spending so much time studying, her schoolwork started to deteriorate too. Then, one day, her mother read an article about heroin in a magazine. Among the illustrations, it showed a picture of the small pieces of charred tin foil that are characteristic of heroin inhalation, and she realized with horror the significance of the identical pieces of tin foil that she had found in Natasha's coat pockets when she had emptied them for washing a couple of weeks before. She decided to confront Natasha as soon as she got in from school that afternoon.

Natasha burst into tears as soon as her mother asked her if she was using drugs. She was worried about it herself . At first it had just been a bit of fun with friends and an escape from the pressure of exams, but now she didn't seem able to stop and she was feeling pretty unwell – she was constipated and her periods had stopped. She had spent most of the money from her savings account, and was worried about what would happen when it ran out altogether.

They went to see her GP together, and Natasha was referred to the local Community Drugs Team. She was prescribed medication to replace the heroin she had been using, and was helped gradually to reduce the dose and stop altogether.

Now that her worries were out in the open, Natasha was able to talk to her mother or to a counsellor about the pressures she felt under at school, and, although it was sometimes difficult, she managed, apart from the occasional relapse, to avoid using heroin again. Several months later, and with her exams behind her, she is finding it easier and easier to cope, and doesn't think that she will fall into the same trap again. 'I wouldn't let myself get so wound up another time. It's better to get worries out in the open and talk about them than to bottle them up inside – I know that now.'

What if I find a substance I think might be an illegal drug?

It has to be said that you are unlikely to find drugs themselves lying around, although if you are really worried, a search of your child's bedroom or possessions might reveal a hidden supply. Any unidentified tablets, powders, crystalline or herbal substances, liquids or even small, printed squares of paper could give cause for concern, although they can be very difficult to identify with any certainty and may be quite innocent. There is always the possibility that your child has been given a substance by a friend and has no intention of using it himself, that he carries it around and shows it to his mates out of bravado, even that he has provided himself with something that looks a bit like a drug for that purpose.

Having found a substance you fear might be an illegal drug, your immediate reaction will probably be to try to find out what it is. You could go about this in several ways.

• *Call a drugs help agency*
For some addresses and telephone numbers, see pages 123-126. Release say that they may be able to make a tentative guess at the identity of a substance described over the telephone, although they would be concerned to talk with the parent about what they would do with the information and help with the wider issues of talking to the child and tackling any drug problem that may exist. The Institute for the Study of Drug Dependence say that they could not offer to identify a suspected drug over the telephone, but would send information that would help parents to make an identification themselves.

- *Ask a pharmacist to identify it.*

Any pharmacist who is a member of the National Pharmaceutical Association (NPA), as 10 000 of the 12 000 pharmacists in the UK are, has access to a comprehensive database of both proprietary and street drugs, which will enable him or her to identify most tablets and capsules. Less easily identifiable substances, like powder, crystals, or resins, may need to be analysed, and, although the pharmacist may be able to arrange this for you or put you in touch with someone who can, it can be expensive.

The NPA say that it is not uncommon for parents to ask their members to identify drugs they suspect their children have been using, and that, thankfully, these usually turn out to be something perfectly innocent, like aspirin or vitamin tablets. If, however, the substance does turn out to be an illegal drug, there is a possibility that the pharmacist may inform the police, although this is unlikely in the circumstances. Both the NPA and the Royal Pharmaceutical Society of Great Britain say that, although pharmacists are bound by a code of ethics that includes the observance of patient confidentiality, it is up to the discretion of the individual to decide what action he or she will take when faced with a situation in which a crime may have been, or is being, committed.

A pharmacist can dispose of some drugs for you, but only if they are drugs that are seen as having therapeutic uses and can be prescribed and dispensed. The pharmacist would be committing an offence if he or she took possession of a drug that falls under schedule 1 of the Misuse of Drugs Act (see Chapter 9).

- *Take it to the police for identification*

The police may be able to identify the substance immediately in some cases, but more often it will be necessary for them to take the substance away for analysis or for expert advice. If it proves to be an illegal drug, they will probably be keen to find out more about where it came from, especially if you have found a quantity that is considered too large for personal use, or if it is one of the more dangerous drugs. Before you go to the police for help with identification, it is worth considering whether it would be helpful to get them involved at this stage or whether you would rather have the chance to find out just how deeply your child is involved in drug use – if, indeed, she is involved at all – before deciding on the best course of action.

- *Ask the child*
It is, admittedly, very difficult to find a way of saying 'I was going through your things while you were out yesterday, and I found this. What is it?' that doesn't provoke fury and accusations of breach of privacy and trust on the part of your child. Taking the substance away for identification, or involving others in the issue before you have spoken to your child, could well make matters worse, however.

If you do decide to talk to your child about what you have found – probably the best course of action in the long run – it is important that you acknowledge his anger, saying, for instance, 'I'm sorry, I wouldn't normally think of doing a thing like this, but I was so worried about the way you've been lately that I looked in your bag/under your mattress/through your pockets and found this. I know that you must be feeling very angry with me, but we really do need to talk about what's been worrying you lately, and I think that this might be important.' Your child may be angry, embarrassed, and afraid of what will happen next, but he does at least know that what you have done was motivated by your concern for him, not by a desire to control him or prevent him from growing up. It reassures him that the boundaries of privacy and trust within your family are still in place and recognized by all of you, even though you may have overstepped them on this occasion.

What should I do with the substance now?
If what you have found does prove to be an illegal drug, it is now technically in your possession, and the safest thing to do

is to destroy it or, if you feel that the situation warrants it, hand it over to the police. If you do not do so, you are, technically, committing the offence of possession. It is now an offence to flush drugs down the toilet or into the public sewerage system by any other means, although this would still be the first reaction of many parents. Consigning dangerous substances to the dustbin or dumping them somewhere is obviously not a sensible or safe option, so you may have to use considerable ingenuity in disposing of suspect or illegal substances. Some parents may feel that they are best handed in at a police station, but avoid awkward questions by saying that they found them somewhere other than in their own home – perhaps that someone threw them over their garden fence, or that they found them in the street, for instance. This is a difficult area, and parents will choose their own way to tackle it, depending on the circumstances and the dictates of their own conscience.

Emergency aid

A few parents only find out about their child's drug use when they find them sick, confused, or unconscious as a result of having used a substance or a combination of substances. It is very unlikely that you will ever have to cope with the consequences of a bad drug experience, but it is useful to know what to do if your child or one of their friends is ever adversely affected by drugs. Your child should know this, too, as she may find herself looking after a friend who has drunk too much or overdosed accidentally at a party, has been given drugs without their knowledge by 'friends', or is in the throes of a 'bad trip' after taking hallucinogenic drugs.

The following pointers are not intended to be a substitute for a first aid course or manual, and it is important that anyone who uses mouth-to-mouth resuscitation or external chest compression has learned to do so properly from a qualified instructor.

If the casualty is unconscious

Ask someone to call for an ambulance. (If you have to do this yourself, do so after you have checked breathing and put the casualty into a safe position.) Check that the casualty is still breathing. If so, loosen any tight clothing, and remove anything that might obstruct breathing, such as a plastic bag or removable dental brace. Place her on her side (in the recovery position if you know it) so that she will not choke if she vomits.

If the casualty is not breathing, lie her on her back on a flat surface and clear the mouth of any obstructions (pills, brace, vomit, and so on). Lift the chin forwards with one hand while pressing the forehead backwards with the other, which will open the airway and may be enough to restart breathing. If it doesn't, and you know how to do it, you will need to try mouth-to-mouth resuscitation. See a first aid manual for further information.

If they are abnormally drowsy

If the person is conscious but very drowsy and you suspect that they have taken drugs, you will need to find out:

- what drug or combination of drugs they have taken
- how – by mouth, inhaled or injected
- how much they have taken
- how long ago they took it

If you are not sure about the safety of the dose or the substance they have used, it is best to err on the side of caution and call an ambulance, or ring the nearest casualty department to ask their advice. If you are sure that there is no immediate danger, the aim is to ensure that the person stays conscious until the effects of the drug have worn off, and to watch them carefully for any signs of deterioration. This could take hours. *Don't* give tea or coffee to help keep them awake, as this will make the drug's effects faster and more intense.

If they are panicking and confused

Certain hallucinogenic and stimulant drugs may cause episodes of panic, confusion, or aggressive and uncontrolled behaviour. If this happens, it is important to remain calm and reassure the person suffering the 'bad trip'. Point out that his feelings are the result of the drug he has used, and will pass, and keep the atmosphere soothing and quiet. This may be enough to calm him down, although it could be a matter of two or three hours before he can safely be left alone.

If he is hyperventilating (overbreathing in rapid, panicky gasps, which can lead to unconsciousness), you can help by encouraging him to breath with you in a slow, regular pattern. Rebreathing air in and out of a paper bag also helps.

If they are having convulsions

Occasionally, drug use, an overdose or withdrawal can lead to convulsions. The eyes will roll upwards and muscles become rigid, followed by twitching and, possibly, loss of bladder control. Put the person undergoing the convulsion into the recovery position, make sure that there is nothing in her mouth to obstruct breathing, protect her head with something soft and ensure that there is nothing around her that she can hurt herself on if she thrashes around. *Don't* jam anything between her jaws or try to hold her tongue down with a spoon or other object as this is not necessary and can cause damage to the teeth.

In all cases

- Collect up anything you can see lying around that might help identify the cause of the problem – pills or other substances, containers, syringes, etc.
- Don't delay getting medical attention because of fears of the police getting involved. This is very unlikely to happen, as medical staff are not obliged to inform the police if they treat an illegal drug user, but, even if they did, it is better to be alive and in trouble than dead and safe from prosecution.

- Don't give anything to eat.
- Don't give coffee, tea, or alcohol, all of which could make matters much worse. Sips of lukewarm water can be given to a conscious casualty who is recovering if he is very thirsty.
- Do keep a careful watch on the affected person for any signs of deterioration. Drug casualties can go downhill very rapidly.

For details of first aid training in your area, look under British Red Cross in your local telephone book.

6
What should I do now?

In most cases, parents will become aware of their child's involvement in drug use before it becomes a serious problem. For a few youngsters, however, it may already be too late to stop easily, although they may by now *want* to stop as much as you want them to. In these cases, it is imperative that parents take a realistic approach and are willing and able to provide the information and support that their child needs in order to manage without drugs. Simply taking the drugs away and stopping them from getting any more, even if it were possible, would not achieve this end. If your child is using drugs regularly and has become psychologically and physically dependent on them, it is imperative that you seek specialist help (see Chapter 7 for details of the help that is available and where to get it).

Immediate reactions

Let's suppose that you have just found out that your child or her group is involved in drugs. Perhaps she, her school, or someone else has told you, or you have found drugs among her possessions. How do you feel? Most parents' first and overwhelming instinct on discovering that their child has used/is using drugs is to make absolutely sure, by any means at their disposal, that they stop immediately and never start again. This is a natural enough reaction, but, unchecked, it can lead to more problems than it solves.

> I waited until he got home from school – about three hours after I found the stuff – and I don't think that I thought about anything else the whole time. By the time he got in I was so wound up I just snapped as soon as he walked through the door. I grabbed him by the arm and screamed that I knew what he'd been up to, how stupid he'd been,

and that he was never ever to bring anything like that into my house again. He turned and ran straight out again

It was a total surprise to be called into the school. We were desperately embarrassed, and couldn't stop apologizing to the headteacher. She must have thought what awful parents we were, not even to know what our child was up to – we were furious with Clare for that.

When we found out that one of his friends had been caught in possession of drugs, we were horrified. He promised us that he had never touched drugs, but his father told him at once that he was forbidden to see that group of friends ever again, and we made sure that he didn't disobey us by checking up on him regularly. It made things pretty uncomfortable at home, but we didn't want to take any chances.

It is natural to be worried – indeed, your child would probably be surprised and anxious if you weren't. You will obviously want to tackle your child about your worries as soon as possible, but it is well worth considering your approach before you leap in with both feet – the eventual outcome may depend on the tone set in the first few minutes of your discussion with your child. As a general guide, try to follow these steps.

- *Calm down*

Difficult though it may be, try to wait until the initial shock and panic have worn off, and you can talk calmly to your child.

- *Choose your moment*

Don't try to talk to your child while he is under the influence of drugs. Wait until you have some time together when you won't be interrupted and neither of you have to dash off anywhere so you can spend as much time as you need.

- *Listen to his side of the story*

It is more helpful, initially, to ask questions than to make assumptions or give lectures. Try, for instance, 'I've heard that some of your friends are taking drugs, and I'm worried that you might get involved. Have you ever been tempted to try any?', or 'We've noticed that you haven't really been yourself lately – you seem to be tired and not very well. Is there something wrong?', or 'I found some things around the house that look like drugs/drug-taking equipment. It worries me to think that you might have been taking drugs, and I'd like to talk to you about it'.

- *Don't make drugs the whole issue*

Drugs are only part of the problem. Ask how your child feels about other things – school, friends, any tensions within the family.

- *Understand that he may find it too difficult to talk to you*

Offer help, support, and advice, but be aware that he may find it easier to talk to someone outside the family. Tell him that you will find sources of help locally (see pages 123-128) and make sure that the information is where he can get at it. Even if he says that he doesn't need help, he may change his mind.

If your child was experimenting with drugs out of curiosity or boredom, which will be the case more often than not, the fact that you have found out and the ensuing discussion may well be enough to discourage him from repeating the experiment. For some children, however, parental opposition will simply make the use of drugs look more attractive as a way of asserting their independence and maturity. You will need to be very careful to avoid making this an issue in which the child feels he must challenge your authority or lose face. This will be easier if you have already talked to your child about drugs in the context of your concern for him and his own self-worth.

Did she want you to know?

Most youngsters are quite capable of keeping from their parents anything that they really don't want them to find out. If you have found evidence of drug misuse around the house or in your child's pockets or bag, it is possible that she wasn't trying very hard to hide them from you. She may have wanted to talk to you about drugs; perhaps she is worried about the risks she has exposed herself to, or feels trapped into drug-taking behaviour she feels uncomfortable with, either by physical or emotional dependency or peer pressure, but couldn't bring herself to approach you direct. Perhaps she wanted to shock you, to assert her independence or to let you know how unhappy she was feeling. In any event, your overreaction could close the door to just the sort of help she is asking for.

You may have heard from another parent, the school, or a contemporary of your child that he is involved with drugs. Alternatively, the signs of possible drug use detailed in Chapter 5 may have tipped you off that something was wrong. In either case, you can't be sure that what you have been told or worked out for yourself is necessarily true. The only person who can tell you for sure is your child. If you go in with both guns blazing, you may never get at the truth.

What next – should I call the police?

You are not obliged by law to report your child to the police, even if you know that they have been taking illegal drugs (see Chapter 9 for more detail about drugs and the law). Some parents, however, do decide to involve the police when they find that their child has been using drugs, and there are two probable reasons for making this decision.

- *To frighten them into stopping*

You may feel that a talking to from the police and the prospect of a criminal record will deter your child from using drugs again. It might, and the police are certainly quite willing to see children and parents in these circumstances. Whether or not they will take action against the child will depend on his age and the type and quantity of drug found (see Chapter 9). If you found the drug yourself and insist on the police prosecuting your child, you will be required to give evidence against him, and it is worth considering seriously whether the effect this might have on your relationship would be helpful or harmful in the long run. For parents who have tried other approaches to their child's continuing drug use, or who feel that he is putting other children in or outside the family at risk, this may be their last resort.

- *To nail the people who have supplied him with drugs*

If your child has been using drugs, someone has been supplying her. This is regarded by the police as a serious offence, and you may feel that it is worth putting your child through some unpleasantness if you can reduce the likelihood of her and other children being supplied with drugs from the same source again. The chances are, of course, that she has been supplied by a friend, and may be unwilling to shop her to the police, but if it is just a question of two mates sharing a joint, the police are unlikely to treat either of them very severely – they are more likely to want to follow their leads back to the source of supply.

- *Who should I contact?*

If you do decide to involve the police, a good first point of contact is the schools liaison officer, a member of the local police force who will be used to talking to children, may know your child and any others involved, and will probably be quite happy to give your child a stiff warning 'off the record' if the circumstances are not too serious. Contacting the drugs squad is more likely to result in an investigation, even if your child is not charged. They will be most concerned with tracing the source of supply of the drugs and may be unwilling to let things drop until they have the information they want.

Should I involve the school?

If you have worries about your school-age child, whether or not the school is directly involved, it is always worth talking with teachers who know your child to see if they can shed any light on the matter. They will know who your child is mixing with at school, how he is coping with his school work, whether there has been any change in his behaviour recently and so on.

If you know or suspect that your child has been taking drugs, or if she has said things that make you suspect that children at her school are involved in drug use, even though your child is not, the school should know of your concerns. Where drugs are being taken or distributed on the premises, the school will be concerned to take swift and effective action, which may involve calling in the police, although they are not obliged to do so – some headteachers prefer to handle the matter internally. Children who have been caught carrying or taking drugs on school premises may well be excluded, temporarily or permanently, depending on the circumstances.

Every school should have a policy on drug use, setting out measures both for prevention and for dealing with any instances that arise. Unfortunately, responsibility for this provision rests with the individual school, although some local authorities may produce guidelines for schools in their area. As in any other area of school life, a well thought out and cohesive policy produced after consultation with staff, parents and pupils, and known to everyone in the school, is the most effective way to tackle the issue of drug misuse. If the staff member you speak to isn't aware of such a policy, then it cannot be effective, even if it does exist.

Should I contact the parents of other children I suspect of taking drugs?

If you think that a group of children, including your own, has been experimenting with drug use, it may be helpful to talk to the parents of some of the other children. You may know them already, in which case it will be relatively easy to express your worries and ask if they have noticed anything untoward. It is *not* a good idea to launch into accusations that their child has been leading yours astray, or to give the impression that you are blaming them for inadequate parenting – a 'we're in this together' approach will produce far better results.

Parents can usefully get together to set consistent standards for their children, share information about drugs and prevention, spread the responsibility for hosting their children's gatherings, and just to talk about their worries and experiences as parents. Knowing your children's friends and their parents is a big factor in protecting them from bad experiences and it makes sense to establish these contacts *before* there is any cause for concern.

7
Who can help?

Worries about drugs can place an enormous strain on everyone involved – the user, his family, and the wider circle of those who care about them can all suffer, directly or indirectly. Whether you have found that your child has had a one-off experience with one of the less damaging and addictive drugs or are living with the day-to-day problems of full-blown dependency, you as parents will benefit from the advice and support of a self-help group or specialist drug service, while your child may need help in dealing with the anxieties that made drug use seem attractive in the first place, as well as practical help in coming off drugs, and staying off. The availability of help varies from area to area, but at least some of the range of services below should be available, wherever you live.

Sources of help

Your family doctor
If you and your child have a good relationship with your GP, she can be a useful source of help with the medical problems associated with drug use. GPs will vary in their willingness or ability to help with the emotional and family problems raised by drug issues, but should be able to refer you to a local child guidance clinic, and provide information about other services locally.

Although it is currently the Government's policy to encourage GPs to treat drug users themselves, family doctors vary in their expertise in this field and in their willingness to undertake the sometimes demanding and long-term treatment of drug users. Some may prefer to refer them to a specialist hospital unit or community drug team.

Child Guidance Service

Your family doctor may refer you to a child guidance clinic, or you can contact them yourself without referral if you prefer. The Child Guidance Service provides help with all sorts of family problems, and is free. You will find your local clinic listed under the name of your local authority in the telephone book.

Youth counselling

Most large towns will have a youth counselling centre. Known simply by their house number, these centres open at times when children and young people are able to attend, and provide free, trained, and experienced counselling for all sorts of problems. Youth counsellors are also available in some schools, although children might prefer that their friends didn't know that they were seeing a counsellor. You can make the first contact with the counselling centre and take your child to counselling sessions, but what passes between counsellor and client is confidential, so don't expect to be kept informed.

Community drugs teams

Community drugs teams offer a free service, providing information, advice, and counselling for drug users and their families. Counsellors will help users to work out a reduction plan, if necessary, and provide the support to see it through. There may also be a doctor available who can prescribe any medication needed to back up the programme. Your family doctor will be able to refer you to your local community drugs team, or you can go straight to them without seeing your doctor first. The health authority for your area will be able to tell you how to contact them.

Street agencies

Many communities, especially in larger towns, have drop-in centres offering free information, advice, counselling and, sometimes, medical help with drug problems. No referral or appointment is necessary.

Drug dependency units
These units are usually situated in a hospital, and provide the same range of services as community drugs teams, along with psychiatric and psychological care. Referral from a GP or community drugs team is usually required.

Self-help groups
As drug abuse is not a particularly socially acceptable problem, drug users and their families are rarely able to talk to friends and family about their anxieties. As a result, they often feel terribly isolated and alone. Self-help groups provide an opportunity for both drug users and their families to talk to others who understand what they are going through and will not judge or criticize, and to share information and resources. Many people find that this support enables them to cope with what would otherwise be an overwhelming situation. Narcotics Anonymous and Families Anonymous (see pages 125 and 126) have groups throughout the UK, and will send details to enquirers. Individual groups are often available locally, sometimes attached to drug help or rehabilitation centres.

Legal help
If your child is in trouble with the law, it is important that you get legal advice as soon as possible. You could contact your own solicitor, if you have one, or find one in the Yellow Pages for your area. One voluntary agency, Release, runs a 24-hour national advice line, which can be particularly useful if your child has been arrested for a drugs offence (see page 124 for details).

Which should I choose?
The sort of help you and your child need will depend on the nature and extent of the problem. It may be that a one-off

experiment with drugs, or even a suspicion that came to nothing, has uncovered problems within your family that have little or nothing to do with drugs at all. While you may still want to get information for your child about drugs, the help you and she need may be easily available from a child guidance clinic or youth counselling agency, and specialist drugs counselling may be unnecessary.

Where established or frequent drug use is a problem, though, specialist drugs services will be better able to provide appropriate help.

How do I find them?

Some of the services mentioned above will be listed in your telephone directory, while your GP, local health authority, Citizens' Advice Bureau or main library will be able to put you in touch with others. If you have any difficulty in tracking down help in your area, the Standing Conference on Drug Abuse (SCODA) publish a comprehensive directory that lists sources of help with drug problems in England and Wales, and another for Scotland, and ADFAM National will provide you with details of help in your area. (See page 123 for further details of these two organisations.)

Whose problem is it anyway?

Sometimes parents who take a child along for help with a behavioural or emotional problem are surprised to find that they are advised to bring other members of the family – often the whole family – along for counselling help, either individually or together. If this happens to you, don't feel that your abilities as a parent are being undermined or criticized, or that you or your other children are being blamed for the problems of the child you sought help for in the first place. The fact is that the family is a complex, interdependent unit, and the behaviour of each member has inevitable consequences for every other member and for the family as a whole. As one family therapist working with the families of drug users puts it,

The family is like a raft floating on the sea – each member takes up a position on the raft to keep it stable and afloat. When one member starts messing around – rocking the boat, in fact – the others are forced to take up new positions to maintain the stability of the raft and prevent it capsizing. We can help that member to resolve his problems and find a new position on the raft, but unless the other members are aware of the changes and also adjust their positions, the raft will still be unstable – the user may even be forced back into drug-taking because this has become his role in the family. With help, however, everyone can find a comfortable and stable place on the raft again.

In short, a problem in the family is everybody's problem, and everybody needs to be involved in the solution.

What if my child doesn't want to be helped?

You can find sources of help for your child, you can even drag her along to see a doctor or counsellor, but unless she wants and is willing to accept the help on offer it will be of little use. Sometimes, especially with older teenagers, your insistence may make it *less* likely that she will take up the help on offer, and some parents may have to accept that the best they can do is to make as much information on sources of help as they can available to the child, and leave it to her to take it up when she feels ready.

The feeling of being powerless to help is often the most difficult thing that the parents and friends of drug users have to cope with, and you may need a good deal of help and support in accepting and living with the long-term nature of some drug and drug-related problems. In the next chapter, we look at ways of helping your child and yourself in the longer term.

8
Longer-term measures

You have found that your child has become involved in drug use. The initial shock has passed, and, perhaps with the help of a doctor or counsellor, you have begun to assess the extent of the problem. It is at this stage that you may have to come to terms with the fact that your child's drug use, or at least the problems leading to and surrounding it, could be with you for a long time to come.

Perhaps your child is unwilling to admit that she has a problem. Perhaps she doesn't want to stop using drugs or, because she has become physically or psychologically dependent on them, is unable to do so even though she wants to. Perhaps she has promised that she will stay away from drugs in future, but you feel that you just can't trust her to stick to that promise. For many parents and their children, there is a difficult and stormy period of adjustment before acceptance and trust can be rebuilt. The experience of Michael's parents, told here by his mother, Carol, clearly illustrates this.

We were devastated when we found that Michael had been smoking cannabis regularly and using other drugs, sometimes even hard drugs like heroin when he and his mates could afford it. He was only 16, but we live on a big estate and he had always had friends within reach and spent a lot of time with them, so we had missed the signs that anything was wrong until the drugs had become a habit. Things were really bad at home for a while after we found out, but after the tears and the shouting on both sides were over and he had promised that he would stay away from drugs in the future, we really believed that he had stopped. We just didn't realize how important the whole thing had become to him, and how difficult it would be for him to resist the temptation to join in when his friends were smoking, or when he was offered drugs and had money in his pocket. It wasn't long before we suspected that he was using drugs again. We would confront him, and he would get angry and accuse us of not trusting him or storm out of the house. He wouldn't come back until late, and we would ring around his friends trying to find him, which made him even angrier. The worry and the rows were making all of us miserable – sometimes it seemed as though we thought of nothing else, but we couldn't talk to our friends and family about it, we were so ashamed. We were watching Michael all the time, wondering: 'Has he used today? Where's he going tonight?' Looking back, the strain on him must have been terrible, as well as the worry for us.

I got so depressed that I went to my doctor for help, and he sent me to a counsellor at our local hospital – she was part of the community drugs team. She understood how I felt, but she explained how hard it was for someone who had got used to using drugs to stop. She said that it was quite normal for it to take a long time for a drug user to be able to give up, and that they almost always had to have several tries and relapses before they were successful. She said that we had to accept that we couldn't *make* Michael stop taking drugs, it had to be because it was what he wanted. I began to realize that the pressure and the rows were actually making it harder for Michael to stop – he needed the drugs to help him escape from the stress and anger he felt and the fear that he couldn't face life without them any more. His father and I talked about all this, and we decided that we had been asking too much of Michael and ourselves. We had made ourselves responsible for his drug use, and worried all the time that if we didn't keep a constant eye on him, he would go back to his old ways. Instead, we talked to Michael and agreed on some ground rules: he would tell us where he was going and what time he would be back, and we wouldn't ring up his friends to check up on him, for instance. We told him that we understood how difficult it was for him to stop using drugs when most of his friends were still using them, and that we were impressed by how well he had done so far, even if he didn't always manage to resist the temptation. We also told him that one of the counsellors at the hospital would always see him if he needed help and put the telephone number in the book by the phone, and, although he didn't say so, I think that he may have seen someone there.

Things didn't get better overnight, but by this stage we didn't expect them to. Michael did seem happier, though, and he began to drift away from his old friends and got involved in a new mountain biking club that started up at the local youth centre. His father paid him a bit to help build a patio in our garden over a few weekends, and helped him find a couple of casual jobs cutting grass and cleaning cars. We were worried at first that he might spend the money on drugs, but it seemed more important to him because he had earned it himself, and he opened a building society account and saved most of it for a new bike. I think that he has more-or-less grown out of drugs now, and I'm sure that the best thing we did to help him was just not to get in the way of that by putting him and ourselves under too much pressure. We were unrealistic to expect it all to be over in a week or two, as we did at the beginning – it's taken well over a year to get this far – but I'm much more confident now in Michael's ability to handle his own problems, which must be what any parent really wants for their child.

Living with someone who is using drugs is hard for anyone, but doubly so for a parent who has to cope with the additional worry that they were somehow responsible for their child's problems, that they failed him in some way during his childhood, or are failing him now in not being able to stop him using drugs. It isn't easy to accept that you can't control or change the situation, but there are ways in which you can help your child, even though you can't make the problem go away immediately.

Coming off

The difficulty of breaking an established drug dependence should never be underestimated, and it is perfectly normal for someone who seems totally committed to ending her habit to have several failures before she succeeds in becoming drug-free. This is hard enough for the dependent individual to handle, but may cause immense problems for those around her, who find it very difficult to understand her failures and feel personally betrayed when she slips back into drug use. It is worth remembering the following points.

- The user will only manage to break free of drugs when she wants to do so badly enough *for herself.* This doesn't mean that she doesn't care about the effects that her drug use is having on those around her, but, in the end, that is not enough to make the enormous effort required to end dependency possible. She will only achieve a drug-free life if this is what she truly wants for herself.

- Putting pressure on the user to end his habit before he is ready may actually *prolong* his drug use. You don't have to pretend that you are happy about the situation, but making his life a misery with constant emotional scenes and accusations of ruining your life may make him feel so bad that he can only escape from his depression and anxiety by taking more drugs.

- Escaping from a drug habit is a long process. When she does slip up, as she almost certainly will, her confidence in her own ability to manage without drugs will take a knock. She will need support and encouragement to try again, rather than accusations of not trying or assumptions of failure.

• Drug users often put those who care about them in impossible situations. When you care about someone, you don't want to see them suffer, but beware of doing anything that allows the user to escape from the consequences of their drug use. As one experienced drugs counsellor says, 'Don't expend too much effort in trying to keep your child out of trouble. Sometimes it is necessary for him to sink to the bottom and swirl around there for a while before he realizes that it isn't where he wants to be'.

• Don't lose sight of your own needs. Sacrificing your happiness and well-being to look after a dependent child who makes no contribution to the family will do neither of you any good. Your child may not be able to stop using drugs for the time being, but her dependence should not become an excuse for bad behaviour. Agree boundaries within which she must operate: she must agree not to steal from you or ask you to pay for her habit, abuse or hurt members of the family while under the influence of drugs or drink, and to see a counsellor regularly, for instance. Make it clear that she can only stay if she keeps up her end of the bargain.

Treatment for addiction.

There are several methods of tackling established addiction, and, once the user has decided that this is what he wants to do, he will need to talk over the alternatives with an experienced drugs counsellor or doctor to decide which will be best for him. The main alternatives are as follows.

Maintenance on prescribed drugs
Some of the dangers of drug abuse arise from the illicit nature of the drug – adulteration with other substances,

variable purity and strength, the administration of the substance by means for which it was not manufactured – and the pressure to finance what soon becomes a very expensive habit by dubious means. These dangers can be largely overcome if the user seeks medical help for his addiction and is prescribed substitutes for the drug he is dependent on – an approach taken mainly with opiate drugs. The aim of these maintenance programmes is to stabilize the user's habit until such time as he is ready to embark on a reduction programme or detoxification, and he will usually be offered counselling or psychiatric help in the interim.

Reduction programmes

In conjunction with a doctor or counsellor, the user may decide to reduce the dose of either the drug she has been using or a substitute drug in planned steps, until she reaches a point where she can stop taking it altogether with a minimum of unpleasant withdrawal symptoms. It is important that she receives counselling and support throughout the programme, and that she feels able to go back to her doctor and counsellor to renegotiate the reductions if she finds them too hard to stick to or doesn't manage to achieve her target in the time they negotiated.

In-patient detoxification

Detoxification involves complete withdrawal of the drug so that it is eliminated from the body entirely, and the physical effects of dependency are reversed. There are some, though very few, in-patient detoxification centres in the UK, where patients can be detoxified under medical supervision, and with the help of drugs that minimize the discomfort that withdrawal inevitably causes. The worst of the effects will probably be over in a few days, but the detoxified individual may feel ill and weak for some considerable time afterwards, and may not feel really well again for some six months or so.

Home detoxification, with or without medical help

It is possible to detox at home, either under the supervision of a doctor or without medical support (although this would be unwise where there has been heavy drug use over a long period). It is important that the user has someone on hand who knows what to expect and can keep an eye on him, as he may become quite ill and confused for a time.

Rehabilitation

Although detoxification may seem like the answer to drug dependency, it is really only the start of the recovery process. Although the drug itself is often the focus of concern for the addict and his family, it is important to remember that it is, in itself, not the problem, but the user's way of coping with it. Unless the factors that made drug abuse attractive are addressed and resolved, there will inevitably be relapse or transference to some other form of dependence.

Someone who has learned to use drugs in this way will need a great deal of ongoing help and support if he is to discover new ways of coping without drugs. Hazel, whose 20-year-old son, Adam, stopped using opiates after three years of dependency, found that her relief was short-lived.

> For so long, my every waking moment was filled with the conviction that if he could just stop taking the drugs everything would be all right. I felt that we could cope with anything if only we didn't have this constant worry about where he was, what he was doing, where he was getting the money to buy the drugs and so on. Three weeks after his detoxification, I actually found myself thinking that it might have been easier if he'd just stayed on the drugs after all.
>
> It was a nightmare – he felt ill all the time, his nerves were raw, he was hell to live with. The worst thing was that getting and taking the drugs had become such a big part of his life that he really seemed lost without it. He just

wandered around aimlessly, complaining about how ill he felt, getting irritable with everyone or depressed. He was so demanding – he couldn't sleep and would get up in the middle of the night and crash about in the kitchen or turn the television on, waking everybody else up, he wanted sympathy all the time. We really hadn't expected any of this – I suppose that we just thought he would stop taking drugs, and that from that point on things would return to normal.

We all needed a lot of support to get us through that difficult time and, luckily, we found it through a Families Anonymous group. Fortunately, things did start to get better. Adam settled down and started to discover ways of handling his feelings with the help of a counsellor, but I think it took four or five months before we really began to feel that he was finding his feet. We just didn't understand the depth of his problem – we only saw the consequences of his drug use, not the reasons for it. I'm sure that the same must happen to a lot of families.

Anything that helps the ex-user to establish a new way of life without drugs will help in his rehabilitation. As Adam found, part of the problem will be simply filling the void left by the business of getting and using the drugs themselves. For many dependent individuals, this takes up a large proportion of their waking hours, and the effect of ending it can be rather like the effect of retirement on someone who has worked a nine to five day all their lives. If you can help him to fill that void with some activity or interest, you will be going a long way towards keeping him safe from future drug use.

Counselling and other forms of therapy can also be helpful in building an understanding of, and a positive attitude towards, the problems that led to drug abuse in the first place. The need for help is not over just because the drug use is – indeed, it may be greater than ever.

Residential rehabilitation

There are a number of centres for residential rehabilitation throughout the UK. The approach taken varies, but most require that the resident be drug-free on admission. The principal of this approach is to help the resident establish a new way of life without drugs. Some will take a religious approach to the problem, others will base their approach on the '12 step' method associated with Alcoholics and Narcotics Anonymous, and many will use a variety of methods of group and individual support to help residents towards a drug-free life.

Most people who take this route spend between a year and 18 months in residential rehabilitation, although some centres provide shorter programmes, backed up by ongoing non-residential support for the user and his family. The cost may be met by social security, the local authority, probation service, charitable funds, or a combination of these, although some centres charge fees to the residents or their families.

Don't give up

An established drug habit can be very hard to break indeed. Often, there will be many setbacks before the user can make the permanent adjustment to a drug-free life, but with the right sort of help most will manage it eventually – often because they have simply outgrown the need for drugs. Some dependent individuals, particularly opiate users, manage to carry on a fairly normal life while they work through their problems, despite their dependency – particularly when they are being maintained on prescribed substitutes.

If you are living with or care for someone who uses drugs, it is all too easy to lose sight of your own needs and focus solely on their problems, but it is vitally important that you seek help and support for yourself, not just for the user, from a counsellor or support group. In the long run, helping yourself will also help your child.

Should I change my child's school?

It is particularly hard for a child to say no to drugs when all her friends are using them, and in some areas and some schools drug use may be almost the norm. As one of the factors that leads to drug use among children is simply exposure to and availability of drugs, choosing your child's school carefully could be an important factor in protecting her from this exposure. When you look at local secondary schools for your child, as well as the questions about exam pass rates and facilities, it makes sense to ask about the school's policy on drugs education and their procedure for dealing with suspected drugs use within the school.

The situation is more difficult where your child has already started at the school and has either reported that drugs are available there, or has had a brush with drug use already. Uprooting a child from school and starting again in another is a serious step, and often very unpopular with the child concerned. It is well worth talking to the school about your worries first. Certainly, I would be more inclined to stay with a school that showed its ability to handle drug-related problems effectively when they did arise than move my child to one where they didn't acknowledge that drugs could be a problem at all within their school. It is a sad fact that all schools will have some pupils who are involved with drugs, whatever parents and staff would like to believe, and that it won't take long for the entire pupil population to know who they are and what they are using. The fact that your child passes this information on to you, while it provides a good opportunity to talk about the risks of drug taking, shouldn't cause you undue panic.

Should we move house?

Statistics on levels of drug availability and abuse among the young show enormous regional variation, with some areas, and even individual estates, becoming well known as drug use 'black spots', in which the risk of any individual youngster encountering and trying drugs is much higher than the national average. Most parents living in an area like this will wish that this was not the case, but moving away is often not possible, and uprooting the family from its familiar environment and dumping it in the middle of a community in which it has no established place may, anyway, cause more problems than it solves.

The factors that make drug abuse more likely in some areas than others are not confined simply to easy availability and the influence of peers. All sorts of social factors affect drug use – unemployment, poor housing, inadequate or absent leisure facilities, and a host of other deficiencies can lead to a situation where a community becomes depressed and hopeless for the future. Young people are affected by this just as much as anyone else, and the result is a rise in drug use and, often, a linked rise in crime. Parents can help to protect their children from these depressing influences both on an individual and a community-wide level by providing them with activities that give them something to work for – sports and youth activity groups are particularly good for this – and by encouraging them to feel that they have a contribution to make to their school, their community, and their future.

In areas where drugs are a major worry for parents, it can be very helpful for them to get together as a group and decide what they are going to do to protect their children. Positive Prevention Plus is a charitable group dedicated to encouraging community awareness and prevention of drug problems among the young, and has developed an effective system of workshops to help parents inform and protect their children. These workshops can be run by all sorts of local groups – PTAs, churches, community centres, or just groups of interested parents – and can provide parents with the confidence and information they need to help their children avoid drug problems. (For their address, see page 125.)

When a community gets together to protect its most precious resource, its children, there are enormous benefits to be had, not just for the children but for all, from the positive feelings that community action generates.

Living with worry and suspicion and rebuilding trust

Even where a child's brush with drugs has been relatively minor and transient, it can leave parents shaken and distrustful. It is as though you have discovered that your child is not the person you thought he was – no longer an innocent child, but a wily teenager who might fall into all sorts of bad ways if he is not watched constantly. For your child, too, there may be a feeling that the boundaries have shifted, that you no longer trust him and that he is expected to do the worst rather than the best in any given situation. As we saw from Michael's story, this can place an enormous strain on all concerned.

Where this happens, it is important that parents and children together renegotiate the boundaries and rules of family life. Expectations need to be examined and restated on both sides, and a workable arrangement arrived at and agreed on by everyone. This isn't as complicated as it sounds. You need to know, for instance, that your child will always let you know where she is going and when she will be home, and that she will stick to the agreed curfew unless special arrangements have been made. She needs to know that you trust her to stick to these arrangements, and that she will be involved in any decisions about matters that affect her. She also needs to know that she can call on you for help if she gets into a situation she doesn't feel happy about, without fear of recriminations or blame on your part. How you arrive at these ends is a matter for negotiation between you, your child, and the rest of the family.

It is hard enough to see your children becoming independent from you, but it is made much harder if expectations are not voiced and boundaries are not defined. You can give your children a far better chance of living up to your expectations, and you to theirs, if everyone is clear

71

about what those expectations are in the first place. There will be occasions, of course, when one of you lets the other down, but if you are all clear about what is really important in your family, it is far less likely that these lapses will involve the really important things that endanger your child's future, his health or your long-term relationship.

Damage limitation

If your child can't or won't stop using drugs, you can at least help to make sure that he uses them as safely as possible. This may feel like admitting defeat to some parents, who naturally want an end to the whole situation, but there are times when parents just have to accept that this isn't going to happen, at least for the time being. Professional help is especially important where there is continued drug use, particularly of the more dangerous drugs and means of administration. The agencies listed in the previous chapter will be able to help here by providing counselling, advice, reduction programmes, and, sometimes, safer substitutes for street drugs, and syringe and needle exchange for users who inject.

Your child may refuse to seek or accept professional help, perhaps because she fears that she will be made to stop taking drugs and just doesn't feel ready to do so. This will not happen. Reduction and detoxification programmes are a matter for negotiation between the user and the professional offering to help them, who knows very well that no one will stop using drugs until they are ready to do so. Nevertheless, if your child doesn't want to get help, you can at least see that she is well informed about the potential dangers of her drug use and ways of making it safer, including:

- the effects of each drug, its addictive potential in its various forms, and its possible side-effects (see Chapter 10)
- the dangers of using adulterated street drugs (see pages

64-65 and Chapter 10) and the existence, on prescription and as part of a treatment programme, of safer substitutes in some cases (see page 65)

• the special dangers of injecting (see page 13)
• the existence of syringe and needle exchange schemes, and the proper cleaning and use of injecting equipment (information can be obtained from local agencies and from the organizations listed on pages 123-126).

While you may have to accept that you cannot stop your child from using drugs, you don't have to pretend to like it, and you certainly shouldn't relieve him of the responsibility for his decision to carry on using. This may involve you in some very hard decisions. If your child comes home stoned and passes out on the living-room floor, do you carry her upstairs to bed, or do you put her in the recovery position and leave her there to wake up cold and stiff in the early hours? Do you rush to the police station and bail your son out when he has been picked up drunk again after a party, or leave him there for the night to think it over? Do you make excuses for your daughter when she is too stoned to get to school or work, or leave her to sort things out for herself? Ultimately, do you allow your child to stay under your roof at your expense when his drug-related behaviour makes life unbearable for the rest of the family, or do you tell him to modify his behaviour or leave?

Before a habitual drug user can move on from using drugs to more mature ways of coping with life, she must accept responsibility for herself and the way she behaves. This doesn't mean that she doesn't need help – she may need it very badly – but she doesn't need the sort of help that allows her to avoid facing up to the effects that her drug use is having on her and those around her. It is especially hard for parents, who have spent their child's lifetime protecting her from situations in which she might suffer harm or distress, to watch her get into situations like those above without stepping in to 'rescue' her, but it is all too easy to prolong your child's drug use by shielding her from its harsher consequences. You will probably need considerable support and guidance if things reach this stage, so don't try to go it alone – contact one of the support agencies mentioned in Chapter 7 and listed on pages 123-126.

A positive outcome

As we have seen, there may be no immediate solution to the family problems surrounding drug use. It may take enormous forbearance and resourcefulness on the part of parents just to avoid making the situation worse, but, ultimately, even the most negative-seeming situations can eventually have a positive outcome, as Helen's story shows.

Alan, who tells Helen's story below, is a policeman. He and his wife, Sandra, have two children – Helen, now 22, and David, two years younger. Problems with Helen began when she was 17 years old.

She started going out with this boy – well, young man really, he was four years older than her – Derek. He was every parent's nightmare: long, greasy hair, scruffily dressed, no job – you know the sort of thing – but she was completely stuck on him. She had been a great kid up to that point; a normal teenager, of course, but no real problems. When they went out together, she would come home late and obviously the worse for drink, and we suspected that she was taking drugs. Right from the start, we had taken a decision always to be honest with our children. Even when they were toddlers, a duck was a duck, not a quack-quack, and a cat was a cat – a pussy cat, maybe, but a cat. When the time came, we took the same approach to subjects like sex and drugs – we told them the truth, in whatever terms they were able to handle at the time. She knew the dangers of drugs and alcohol, but this boy was so important to her that she obviously felt it was worth taking some risks in order to be part of his life.

It wasn't long before she announced that she was leaving home and moving in with him. Sandra and I were horrified, and, of course, we tried to persuade her that it wasn't a good idea, that she should wait a bit longer and see how she felt. She was adamant, however, and it soon became clear that we weren't going to dissuade her. We spent a long time talking about the situation and in the end we decided that, as nothing we could do would change her mind, the best thing that we could do was to be there for her if ever she needed us. It wasn't easy, but we told her that we understood that she had made her decision, but that there was always a room for her at our home if she needed it, and that we wanted her to keep in touch.

The next four years were a nightmare. Derek drank and took drugs heavily, and didn't work. Helen supported both of them, and was obviously involved in drugs as well, although she never became as dependent as Derek did. She lost weight and looked permanently exhausted. She wasn't just working, she was doing all the cooking, cleaning, shopping, and everything else – Derek never lifted a finger around their flat. It was a terrible time for both of us, but worse for Sandra. As a police officer, I knew just how bad things could get – you see it all in the police force – but she just didn't know that people lived like this. Despite it all, we managed to keep a reasonable relationship with Helen. We didn't lecture her about her way of life, we even managed to bite our tongues about Derek, and she continued to see us regularly. She couldn't have kept on like that for ever, though, and eventually the cracks began to show.

It must have been hard for her, but after four years with him she left and came back home. That was a year ago, and the details of their life together are only just coming out – the drinking, the drugs, the way he treated her. I'm just waiting for the three-in-bed stories – I'm sure it's coming. She doesn't drink much or take drugs now – it was just something that she did because she wanted to fit in. I'm so glad that she had the sense to avoid getting hooked on anything, and that she had the strength of character to use substances like alcohol and drugs for a while and then stop. We have managed never to say 'I told you so', even though it would have been easy to do so, and we are just so relieved that we gave her the space to realize that she had made a mistake and get out of that situation before it was too late. Our only real regret, and hers, is that she missed out on those teenage years when she should have been having fun and learning about life – she spent them working her fingers to the bone for that idle swine, Derek. On the other hand, her brother, David, who knew about most of what was going on, has learned a lot from her mistakes. He has seen at first hand the damage that can come from that sort of lifestyle, and I don't think that he is likely to make the same mistakes himself. Sandra and I feel that we made the right decisions under difficult circumstances, and we're glad that we were able to stick by them – it paid off in the end.

9

Drugs and the law

The use of drugs in the UK is controlled by the Misuse of Drugs Act 1971. For the purposes of this Act, drugs deemed likely to be misused are divided into three categories – A, B, and C, graded according to the possible dangers attached to the misuse of the individual drug. Offences involving class A drugs – those deemed to be the most dangerous – attract higher penalties than those in classes B or C, which are perceived as being less dangerous in their effects. As new drugs appear on the scene, they can be included by the Home Secretary in the list of those covered by the Act, without referral to Parliament.

The Act is further qualified by five Schedules, which define who may legally prescribe, handle, or distribute drugs, and in what form, according to their possible legitimate medical use. The descriptions of drugs listed in Chapter 10 include details of their status under the Misuse of Drugs Act, but the list below will give you a general guide to the sorts of drug included in each class.

Class A drugs
These include cocaine, diconal, heroin, LSD, methadone, morphine, opium, ecstasy and cannabinol (the active ingredient of cannabis resin extracted and sold separately – an extremely unusual occurrence).

Class B drugs
These include amphetamines, cannabis and cannabis resin, codeine in concentrations above 2.5 per cent, DF118, ritalin, and barbiturates. Class B drugs can fall under class A, though, if they have been prepared for injection.

Class C drugs
These include benzodiazepines and methaqualone.

The penalties
Penalties for possession and for supply or trafficking vary with the class of the drug concerned, with class A drugs attracting a maximum penalty of life imprisonment and an unlimited fine for trafficking, while possession of a class C drug may result in a few months in prison or a fine of a few hundred pounds. These penalties do, however, change from time to time. For the latest information, contact Release (see page 124 for their address and telephone number).

It is, in fact, quite legal to possess some class C drugs, provided that they are for medicinal use. These qualifications are laid down in the Act's five schedules, which classify drugs broadly as follows.

• *Schedule 1*
Drugs with no recognized legitimate therapeutic purpose, such as cannabis or LSD. Only those who have been issued with a Home Office licence, usually for research purposes, may legally possess these drugs. They cannot be prescribed by doctors or dispensed by chemists.

• *Schedule 2*
This covers drugs that are considered to have some legitimate medical use. These drugs may be possessed by doctors, pharmacists, scientific researchers, and analysts, and some nursing staff, providing that they are employed in hospitals or nursing homes. It is legal for someone who has been prescribed one of these medicines to have it in his possession, provided that it is used according to the instructions given by the doctor. This category includes heroin, morphine, amphetamine and cocaine.

- *Schedule 3*

As schedule 2, but covering less powerful drugs like slimming aids.

- *Schedule 4*

Schedule 4 drugs may be possessed by any of the people listed under schedules 2 and 3, who may also supply them to others. If they are included in a medicinal product, they may be possessed, although not supplied, by anyone. Drugs in this schedule include commonly used benzodiazepines like Temazepam and Lorazepam.

- *Schedule 5*

Many medicinal preparations like cough mixtures and anti-diarrohoea medicines contain very small amounts of controlled drugs, and these are covered by schedule 5. Some may be sold over the counter, without a prescription, and they can all be possessed legally, even without a prescription. They cannot, however, be supplied to another person once they have been bought.

Unclassified substances

Some substances, such as solvents and butyl nitrite, both substances open to misuse, are not classified as drugs at all and, therefore, are not covered by the provisions of the Misuse of Drugs Act and its schedules. In the case of solvents, special legislation has been introduced to make it illegal to sell them to anyone under 16, knowing or suspecting that they may be used for the purpose of inhalation.

Is my child doing anything illegal?

If your child has experimented with controlled drugs, it is probable that he has committed an illegal act, although in practice it is quite unlikely that a child or adolescent who has had a passing acquaintance with drugs will end up with a criminal record. Anyone possessing, supplying, producing, trafficking in, importing or exporting a controlled drug may be in breach of the law. The offences of possession and supply are the most likely of these to apply to a young person experimenting with drugs, and it is important that you and your child know just where the line between possession and supply is drawn, as both the likelihood of prosecution and the possible penalty are markedly higher if he is supplying drugs than if he possesses them solely for personal use.

Possession

Drugs don't have to be in your physical possession, that is, in your pocket or handbag, for the offence of possession to have taken place. Leaving drugs somewhere for collection later on, say under your mattress or with a friend, also qualifies as possession. On the other hand, someone taking a drug that it would be illegal for her to possess to someone who is entitled to have it, for example, collecting your granddad's tranquillizer prescription from the chemist, is not an offence. A parent finding a substance in their child's bedroom and taking them to the police would not be committing the offence of possession, neither would a teacher taking drugs away from a pupil in order to destroy them.

Strangely, the law allows for a person to be charged with possession of what they believe to be a controlled drug, even if it turns out on analysis to be another substance altogether. If a teenager buys a substance at a disco that he is told is cocaine, and when challenged by the police 'admits' is cocaine, but which later turns out to be another drug or even some other innocuous substance, he may still be charged with possession of cocaine because he believed that this was what he was carrying.

Being in the same place as people who are taking drugs, even if you know about it, does not amount to the offence of possession, but a group of people who are sharing a common supply of a drug – passing a joint of cannabis around at a party, for example, can all be guilty of possession.

An offence of possession may have been committed even if the quantity of drugs found is so small as to be unusable, although prosecutions involving only traces of drugs can be difficult to pursue. Traces of drugs found in urine or blood samples, however, cannot be used as evidence for a charge of possession.

Supply

Supplying drugs is viewed as a much more serious offence than possession, and it comes as a surprise to many people that you don't actually have to sell drugs to anyone in order to be charged with supplying.

With drugs like cannabis available at pocket-money prices, many young people will share them among their friends. Even giving a friend a few puffs of your joint could be said to be supplying, and giving her enough to roll her own, even though no payment is asked for or given, will lay the giver open to criminal charges. Handing back to a friend drugs that have been left with you for safekeeping is also considered to be supplying.

Possession with intent to supply is a common charge. If the quantity of drugs found in an individual's possession is obviously too large for personal use, the inference will be that the excess is intended for supply to others. If one person undertakes to buy drugs for a group of people, who give him their money for the purchase, he will still be seen as supplying the others, even though he is buying the drugs for their use and with their money.

Other offences

Production of controlled drugs, although not a specific offence in its own right, can be prosecuted under drug trafficking laws or it may be treated as a less serious offence, depending on the circumstances. Growing cannabis is an offence, as is cultivating hallucinogenic (magic) mushrooms for the purpose of using psilocybin, the hallucinogenic substance found in them.

Import and export

The import and export of drugs are covered by complicated legislation, mostly designed to prevent large quantities of drugs being moved from country to country for commercial purposes. Carrying controlled drugs through customs is obviously unwise, and will result in prosecution if you are caught. Less obviously, someone receiving a parcel containing drugs from a friend abroad, even if they didn't know that it was coming, could be accused of importing the drugs if they kept them. The safest thing to do to avoid prosecution in these circumstances would be to destroy the drugs immediately.

Drug-taking equipment

Possession of drug-taking apparatus is not illegal, although the supply and distribution of it may be. The presence of such apparatus could be used in conjunction with other evidence to support a prosecution for a drug offence, however.

What will happen if my child gets caught?

The law treats children differently from adults, and the extent to which a child can be held legally responsible and accountable for her actions varies with her age. Anyone under 17 years of age is legally defined as a juvenile, and within this category children are further divided into three distinct age groups for the purposes of prosecution and sentencing.

- *Aged under 10*

A child under ten years old cannot be found guilty of any criminal offence, and is immune from prosecution. If a child in this age group persistently breaks the law, however, he may be taken into local authority care.

- *Aged 10 to under 14*

A child in this age group can be tried and found guilty of a criminal offence, although it must be shown that she knew she was doing wrong. While she can be found guilty of most of the same offences as an adult, she will be tried in a juvenile court, and the penalties imposed by the court will be different – usually involving restrictions on where she lives and how she behaves, enforced attendance at school, and regular supervision and counselling.

- *Aged 14 to under 17*
While still classified as a juvenile, a child in this age group is expected to take responsibility for any criminal act he performs. It is no longer a defence to show that he didn't know that he was breaking the law. If prosecuted, he will still be tried in a juvenile court, but may now be sentenced to detention in a young offenders institution if the seriousness of his offence is thought to merit a custodial sentence.

The penalties
Even where a criminal offence has clearly been committed, the police have a good deal of discretion in deciding whether or not a prosecution should be brought. If a juvenile admits guilt, they can decide to caution her instead of proceeding with a prosecution. This is not the same as just giving her an informal talking to, which an officer investigating an incident involving drugs may decide to do whether the child admits guilt or not. While an official caution issued to a juvenile does not go on to a criminal record, it is noted and can be referred to if the child appears before a juvenile or criminal court in the future. There is no limit to the time for which a caution may be held on police records.

What actually happens if the school or police catch a young person in possession of drugs, therefore, will depend on the classification of the drug involved, the quantities they are carrying, the circumstances of the case, and the age of the child or young person involved. Schools will often be reluctant to call in the police and may contact parents first. Where the police are involved and the youngster is under 17, and where there is no history of drug use or general antisocial behaviour, the probable outcome will be a stiff talking to or a caution. Only in cases where quantities of drugs too large for personal use are involved or where the drug found is of a particularly dangerous nature is there likely to be a prosecution.

While the police may not be interested in prosecuting your child, they may be very interested to know where they got the drugs from. The main concern the police have is to cut off the lines of supply rather than to tackle individual drug users.

Will I be prosecuted if the police find drugs in my house?

It is illegal to allow drug production or supply in premises that you occupy or to allow the use of cannabis or opium. If you own a house but do not occupy it – if, for example, you let a house to students – you are not held legally responsible for drugs offences committed on the premises.

If the police find drugs other than cannabis or opium in your child's bedroom, therefore, you will not have committed any offence, even if you knew that she was using these drugs on the premises and allowed her to do so. If she has been smoking cannabis or opium on the premises it is extremely unlikely that the police will attempt to take any action against you, although you will technically have committed an offence under the Misuse of Drugs Act.

Where people share premises – three students sharing a flat, for instance – if one uses cannabis on the premises with the knowledge of the others, the others can be charged with allowing the flat to be used for smoking cannabis.

What can the law do to protect my child?

As you can see from this brief outline of the Misuse of Drugs Act, the main thrust of the law and concern of the police is to prevent drugs entering the country or being manufactured or distributed here. They will be very keen to know of anyone who is supplying drugs to young people, including shopkeepers and publicans who sell solvents, alcohol, or tobacco to underage customers, and will welcome your help and your child's in bringing a prosecution against such people. It is very unlikely that your child or her friends will end up with criminal records as a result of your reporting incidents to the police or passing on information themselves, unless they have become heavily involved in dangerous drugs or are dealing – they are not the ones the police are after.

The police also have a role to play in drugs education. Schools liaison officers vary in the amount of coverage they give to drug use in their talks to schoolchildren, but most will at least give an outline of the law, for example, explaining the difference between possession and supply of controlled drugs.

What are my child's rights if suspected or accused of a drug offence?

Police may stop and question anyone they wish whenever they wish. If, as a result of their questioning, they have 'reasonable suspicion' that an offence may be involved, they may conduct a search, with or without the consent of the person they propose to search. Without 'reasonable suspicion', they may conduct a personal search only with consent. Grounds for 'reasonable suspicion' include unusual behaviour, information received and the time or place of activity, but not the way the suspect is dressed, their race or colour, or any knowledge the police may have of previous drugs convictions.

According to the rules governing searches, a search with consent can be more detailed than one without. If the search is to be more than a superficial inspection of outer clothing, it must be taken by a police officer of the same sex as the suspect. In cases where a drugs offence is suspected, police may take the suspect to a police station for a detailed or intimate search without making a formal arrest.

Intimate searches, involving the examination of body orifices, can only be undertaken by a doctor or nurse in a hospital or clinic, and only when authorized in writing by a police superintendent where there is suspicion that a class A drug has been concealed with criminal intent. Intimate body samples, such as blood, semen, and tissue, and swabs from body orifices, may only be taken with consent, by a doctor, and with written authorization from a police superintendent. Fingernail scrapings, hair, and footprints may only be taken without written consent if authorized by a police superintendent and where there are reasonable grounds to suspect involvement in a serious arrestable offence.

What does a criminal record mean?

The length of time for which a conviction stays on record is governed by the Rehabilitation of Offenders Act 1974. The period before a conviction is considered 'spent' and, therefore, dropped from the record is halved for people under 18, but may still amount to several years. There are three main areas where a criminal record can prove a decided disadvantage:

- future brushes with the law, where a record can influence the outcome of a subsequent case
- going abroad - it can be very hard to gain access to some countries after a drugs conviction
- getting a job - a prospective employer may be very reluctant to take on someone with a criminal record. Some jobs are exempt under the Rehabilitation of Offenders Act, and for those applying for such jobs some convictions are never considered spent, so a prospective employer will always be able to find out about convictions, however far in the past they may have been.

In view of these points, it is worth considering just what a burden a criminal record could prove for many years to come before you decide to involve the police in your child's drug problems.

10

Drugs In More Detail

This section is devoted to hard facts about commonly used drugs and other substances. I have included alcohol and tobacco in the list, as they are two of the most widely used and dangerous drugs in our society, legality notwithstanding. The way we parents, who have grown up with them as an accepted part of our culture, tend to view their risks can give us an insight into the way that our children's generation looks on the risks of 'their' drugs. We may feel that 'they're all right as long as you use them sensibly', 'the only people who become alcoholics are those who already have problems', or 'so-and-so's been smoking for years and he's never had a day's illness in his life', but these rationalizations may equally be applied by our children to other drugs. It pays to look at them again with an open mind before we try to make these justifications to our children about our own habits or reject them when made about theirs!

For each drug in this section, I have listed information on how it is used and what effects it is likely to have in varying doses. While these facts make uncomfortable reading, they will help children to make realistic decisions about drug-taking, and help parents to identify possible drug problems.

Tranquillizers (downers)

Benzodiazepines
- *Legal status*

Prescription only, class C controlled drugs.

- *What are they?*

Benzodiazepines are what is known to the medical profession as 'minor tranquillizers', often prescribed to relieve anxiety or help the patient sleep. Most are marketed in the form of pills or capsules containing powder, with the exception of Temazepam, which comes as a capsule containing gel. All benzodiazepines are classed as prescription-only drugs, and it is illegal to sell or supply them except in this way, but it is not illegal to possess them without a prescription, unless they have been produced illicitly.

- *How are they used?*

sBenzodiazepines are usually taken by mouth, with the exception of the gel Temazepam, which is sometimes injected by illicit users, although it is not manufactured for use in this way. Because it is possible to inject it, Temazepam has become popular with drug users as a substitute for opiates like heroin or as an aid to those who are 'coming down' after using stimulants like ecstasy or amphetamine.

- *Effects and symptoms*

Benzodiazepines are depressant drugs. In normal doses they can relieve anxiety without unduly impairing the taker's alertness and ability to carry out everyday tasks, like driving. They do not, however, produce the positive feelings of pleasure or euphoria associated with the use of other drugs. In non-anxious individuals they may have very little pleasurable effect, although Valium can sometimes produce mild euphoria. To the observer, someone who has taken benzodiazepines may appear drowsy and slightly uncoordinated.

- *Dependence potential*

Long-term users of benzodiazepines develop both tolerance (a condition in which they have to take increasing doses of the drug to obtain the same effect) and dependence. This dependence is probably more psychological that physical, resulting in feelings of anxiety and panic if the drug is unavailable. Users who have been taking high doses over a long period may experience physical withdrawal symptoms, such as tremors, nausea, and vomiting, starting several days after stopping the drug and continuing for two or three weeks or more.

• *Dangers*
A fatal overdose is possible, particularly if alcohol has been taken at the same time. Injecting the gel Temazepam, which is not designed to be administered in this way, is a dangerous practice and can result in severe circulatory problems, aside from the inherent risks of injecting any drug. If coordination is affected, tasks such as driving or using dangerous machinery are obviously risky.

Barbiturates
• *Legal status*
Prescription only, class B controlled drugs.

• *What are they?*
Like benzodiazepines, barbiturates have been used medically in the treatment of anxiety and to help the patient sleep. Because they carry a very high risk of fatal overdose, they have been largely replaced in the treatment of all but the most severe cases by the safer benzodiazepines, so are now little used medically and, therefore, not widely available to illicit users.

Barbiturates are supplied as tablets, capsules, solutions, suppositories and ampoules, with coloured capsules being the most common form of the drug.

• *How are they used?*
Barbiturate users usually take the drug by mouth, but may also inject crushed tablets or the powder contained in capsules dissolved in water.

• *Effects and symptoms*
Barbiturates produce effects similar to those produced by alcohol. In small doses, perhaps one or two pills, they can

make the user feel relaxed and sociable. At higher doses the sedative effects tend to take over, and the user becomes dopey, clumsy, and poorly coordinated, with slurred speech. They may also become emotional and confused and, ultimately, fall asleep.

- *Dependence potential*

Physical tolerance develops rapidly with repeated use of barbiturates, so the regular user will have to take increasingly high doses to achieve the same effect. Unfortunately, the potentially fatal dose does not increase much at all with tolerance, so that the regular user may eventually need to take a potentially lethal dose in order to achieve the effect he requires. Psychological dependence is likely, and regular use of high doses can cause physical dependence and severe withdrawal symptoms if the drug is stopped. These can include twitching, irritability, inability to sleep, nausea, and occasionally convulsions. Sudden withdrawal from regular use of very high doses can prove fatal.

- *Dangers*

Barbiturates are extremely dangerous – hence their lack of popularity as a legitimate drug. The dose at which they can cause death through respiratory failure is very low – in fact, at ten or so tablets, the lethal dose is little more than the normal medicinal dose – and they become potentially lethal at even lower doses if alcohol or other depressants have been taken.

Injecting barbiturates is particularly hazardous, with an increased risk of overdose and of gangrene and abscesses over other commonly injected drugs. The sedative effects and lack of coordination caused by the drug can also be dangerous, with an increased likelihood of accidental injury and of hypothermia, caused by the drug's effect on the way the body responds to cold.

Alcohol

• *Legal status*

Licensing laws control the manufacture, sale, purchase, and distribution of alcoholic beverages. It is an offence to give alcohol to a child under five years of age, except for medical purposes. Children under 14 may not enter the part of licensed premises where alcohol is bought and consumed; 14 to 18 year olds may enter but may not buy or drink alcohol. Sixteen year olds and over may buy beer, cider, or perry to drink with a meal (not served at the bar). These restrictions vary slightly in Scotland and Ireland.

It is an offence under the Public Order Act 1986 to carry or possess alcohol on trains, coaches, or minibuses travelling to and from designated sporting events. It is also an offence to be drunk in a public place, to be drunk and disorderly, or to drive while over the legal limit. Beers, wines and cider may be brewed at home without a licence, but not sold.

• *What is it?*

The active ingredient of alcoholic drinks is ethyl alcohol, which is produced by the action of yeasts on grain, fruits, and vegetables (fermentation). Beers and wines have been known the world over throughout history, with various and often less than successful attempts being made over the centuries to limit the use and abuse of alcohol by various groups, usually the working classes and the young.

Methyl alcohol, which is produced from wood and is considerably cheaper than ethyl alcohol, may also be used by alcoholics in the form of methylated or surgical spirit.

• *How is it used?*

Alcohol is invariably taken by mouth in the form of a drink.

• *Effects and symptoms*

At moderate doses (one or two pints of beer or glasses of wine or spirits for most people), the user feels relaxed and sociable. Mental and physical functioning is reduced progressively depending on the amount of alcohol taken, and at higher doses the user becomes uncoordinated, with slurred speech, and may become emotional and/or aggressive. If drinking continues, double vision and loss of balance, and, eventually, unconsciousness will result.

• *Dependence potential*
Tolerance of alcohol develops with repeated use, and the user will have to drink more and more for it to have the same effect. Physical and psychological dependence are very real dangers, and the regular and heavy drinker will experience withdrawal symptoms including sweating, anxiety, trembling and delirium if his supply of alcohol is stopped suddenly. Severe withdrawal can result in convulsions, coma, and death.

• *Dangers*
Regular, heavy drinking can cause stomach, liver, and brain damage. Because it has a high calorific content, drinking can lead to obesity and to dietary deficiencies (where a significant part of the calorific content of the user's diet is replaced by alcohol). The loss of self-control associated with alcohol use can lead to violence and family problems. Alcohol will exaggerate the effects of other depressant drugs such as barbiturates, tranquillizers and solvents, making intoxication and an overdose more likely. As drinking is so much an accepted part of many people's lives, it is more likely than most drugs to be used in conjunction with another.

Solvents
• *Legal status*
It is an offence in the UK (except Scotland) for a retailer to supply a person under the age of 18 with a substance if he knows or has reasonable cause to believe that the substance is or its fumes are likely to be inhaled for the purpose of causing intoxication. In Scotland it is a common law offence to 'recklessly' and knowingly sell solvents to children for the purpose of inhalation.

Anyone driving under the influence of solvents can be charged with the offence of being in charge of a vehicle while unfit through drink or drugs.

- *What are they?*

The substances involved in solvent abuse are carbon-based compounds that either give off vapour or are gaseous at normal temperatures (products commonly containing such compounds are listed in the table on page 117).

- *How are they used?*

Glues (the most commonly misused solvents), are generally put into a plastic bag, and the vapours inhaled through the nose and mouth. Other substances, such as thinners and cleaning fluids, may be inhaled from a cloth or a part of the sniffer's clothing, often a sleeve. Aerosols may be sniffed from bags, but are often sprayed directly into the mouth. Sometimes the user may put her head right into a large plastic bag containing solvents – a dangerous practice (see under Dangers below).

- *Effects and symptoms*

The effect of sniffing solvents is very much like getting drunk on alcohol, but, because the substances used enter the bloodstream more quickly, through the lungs rather than the stomach, they take effect more quickly than alcohol, and also wear off faster. If the sniffer wishes to stay 'high', she will need to keep sniffing – and will sober up quickly once she stops.

As well as the general effect of drunkenness, some sniffers will experience hallucinations. If the atmosphere in which they sniff is unfavourable or they are in a bad mood, these hallucinations may be frightening and unpleasant. Seeing things that aren't really there, or seeing distorted versions of what is really there, may cause the sniffer to do strange and possibly dangerous things, and the fear itself can be dangerous because of the substance's effects on the user's heart (see under Dangers below).

• *Dependence potential*

Physical dependence is not seen as a problem with the use of solvents, although tolerance can develop with persistent use, and the regular sniffer may have to use higher doses to achieve the same effect. Psychological dependence may develop in a few users, usually where there are persistent family or personality problems.

• *Dangers*

Sniffing itself carries dangers, aside from the risks to health from the solvents used. Many sniffers choose hazardous surroundings, such as derelict buildings, where they will not be discovered. Because many of the substances used are highly inflammable, there is a danger of the user setting fire to himself or his surroundings, particularly if he or his companions are smoking. If plastic bags are used, there is a danger that the user may suffocate if he becomes unconscious or choke on his own vomit. If aerosols or butane are sprayed directly into the mouth, they may cause swelling of the tissues in the mouth and throat, blocking the airway and causing suffocation.

The effects on the body of the substances used are difficult to determine. A wide variety of chemicals in varying combinations are involved, in forms and with additives that were never intended for human consumption. It is thought that sniffing can affect the heart, making it more sensitive to exertion or excitement, and that this may be the reason for some of the sudden deaths that have occurred among sniffers. For this reason, it is unwise to subject sniffers to stress during or immediately after sniffing – probably within a few hours – so, chasing after sniffers could obviously be dangerous. The frightening hallucinations that sometimes result from sniffing solvents could also cause the sniffer's body to release adrenaline, which stimulates the heart, and this could be the cause of some sudden deaths of sniffers.

The intoxication resulting from sniffing is similar to the drunkenness caused by alcohol, and the sniffer may fall or do something stupid or dangerous while under the influence of solvents.

Sometimes, although rarely, long-term damage to the body may result from sniffing, including damage to the lungs, heart, kidneys, liver, or central nervous system. Although sniffers have been admitted to hospital suffering from a variety of alarming symptoms, including convulsions, inability to speak or coordinate their movements, and even coma, in most cases these effects have proved to be reversible, and the sufferer has recovered within a day or so. In a few cases, though, highly toxic substances such as the lead in leaded petrol have caused permanent brain damage, or other serious and irreversible consequences.

Stimulants (uppers)

Amphetamines
• *Legal status*
Prescription only, most are class B, controlled drugs, unless in injectable form, when they are classified as class A. The milder amphetamine-related stimulants are classified as class B.

• *What are they?*
Amphetamines are synthetic stimulant drugs supplied in the form of white or yellow powder and tablets. They were used to boost the performance of soldiers in the Second World War and in Vietnam, and were widely used during the 1950s and 1960s as appetite suppressants in the treatment of obesity and to treat depression. As a result of an upsurge in non-medicinal use, they were designated controlled drugs and fell out of favour with the medical profession. They are now rarely used medically.

- *How are they used?*

Most of the illegal amphetamine available to young people is in the form of amphetamine sulphate, an off-white or pink powder, usually composed of a low percentage of amphetamine, adulterated (cut) with other, less powerful stimulants like caffeine or ephedrine. The powder is usually sniffed, but can be injected. Less commonly, amphetamine powders can be dissolved in water and taken by mouth or smoked.

- *Effects and symptoms*

Amphetamines are stimulants, which act on the body in much the same way as the naturally occurring adrenaline. Taken as tablets by mouth and in relatively low doses, they produce a feeling of exhilaration and power, increased energy and ability to concentrate, confidence and the ability to go without sleep or food for long periods. Physical effects can include a rise in blood pressure and increased breathing and heart rates, widening of the pupils, dryness of the mouth, diarrhoea, and increased urination.

Higher doses will produce intensified effects. The user may become very talkative and possibly aggressive, and may appear flushed and sweating. Headaches, grinding of teeth, jaw clenching, and the feeling that the heart is racing can also result.

- *Dependence potential*

Amphetamines do not cause physical dependence or withdrawal symptoms, even after long-term regular use, although there is a rebound effect when the user stops after a run of amphetamine use. Tolerance arises quickly with regular use, however, and increasingly large doses will be required to achieve the same effects. Psychological dependence is a very real risk, and it can be very difficult for the user to stop using amphetamines once he has experienced the sense of energy and well-being induced by the drug, particularly if he is finding life a bit of a struggle. The relapse rate among regular amphetamine users who stop is high.

- *Dangers*

Even at low doses, users can suffer from 'amphetamine psychosis', a condition in which extreme mood swings, irritability, and bouts of uncontrolled and possibly violent behaviour may be displayed. Regular use can mean that this problem becomes serious and persistent, and result in hallucinations and unpleasant sensations of smell, taste, and touch. The sufferer may imagine, for instance, that he feels insects crawling all over him. Although the psychosis fades once the drug has left the body (usually after a few days) it is followed by a rebound effect of extreme tiredness, depression, and anxiety, which may last for days or weeks.

An overdose can result in muscle spasms, racing pulse, and a high temperature. A severe overdose can result in convulsions, coma and, rarely, death from heart failure, collapse of blood vessels in the brain or extremely high fever. Deaths associated with amphetamine use are rare, however, and more usually associated with complications arising from injecting – either from an overdose or AIDS, hepatitis, or the other risks associated with injecting any drug.

Long-term use of amphetamines can lead to high blood pressure, heart problems, and the possibility of a stroke because of the strain it exerts on the heart and circulatory system. Damage to the small blood vessels in the eyes can cause problems with eyesight. Users may fail to eat properly because of the appetite-suppressant qualities of the drug, and may suffer from malnourishment and dietary deficiencies. Women and girls may stop menstruating and become temporarily infertile.

Although the psychosis resulting from amphetamine use passes when the drug is stopped, it is possible that its use may trigger off latent mental illness in even moderate users.

Cocaine

- *Legal status*

A class A controlled drug.

- *What is it?*

Cocaine is extracted from the leaves of the coca bush, which grows in the Andes. It was in popular use as a tonic until 1920, when it was made illegal under the first Dangerous Drugs Act. Supplied either in the form of the crystalline white powder, cocaine hydrochloride, or as freebase, a purer form, or crack, rocky lumps of further processed cocaine, it is a stimulant with properties similar to those of amphetamines.

- *How is it used?*

Cocaine is most commonly sniffed into the nose through a tube, where it is absorbed into the blood through the thin lining. More rarely, it is injected, but it is likely to damage skin tissue and cause ulcers. Freebase cocaine or crack can be smoked, either in cigarettes or pipes, mixed with tobacco, or, more commonly, using a water pipe. Users often make their own pipes, using drinks cans, plastic or glass bottles or drinking glasses, foil and tubing. The drug is heated using a match, DIY-type gas torch or cigarette lighter.

- *Effects and symptoms*

The effects of using cocaine are very much like those of using amphetamines – a feeling of strength and energy, excitement and talkativeness, and a decreased need for food and sleep. Pupils may be dilated and the eyes more sensitive than usual to bright light. Large doses can cause anxiety, aggression, and even hallucinations, which usually wear off once the drug has left the system. If the powder is sniffed, the drug takes effect quickly, peaking within 15-30 minutes. The effects also wear off fast, so the user may have to sniff every 20 minutes or so if she wants to stay high. When the drug is smoked, the effects are almost immediate but last for an even shorter time.

• *Dependence potential*
Cocaine use, even if it is repeated and heavy, does not cause tolerance. After use and as the drug wears off, the user will feel tired, drowsy, and depressed, although these effects are not as great as those associated with amphetamine use. Physical dependence with withdrawal symptoms like those experienced by opiate users is not a problem for cocaine users, even regular ones, but strong psychological dependence is likely for the regular user.

• *Dangers*
Very frequent use can cause unpleasant feelings of anxiety, restlessness, insomnia, nausea, and weight loss due to decreased appetite. The user may become physically and mentally exhausted through lack of sleep. The heavy user may go on to suffer from a condition similar to 'amphetamine psychosis' described above. All these symptoms should clear up if use of the drug is discontinued.

Repeated sniffing can cause ulceration and other damage to the nose. Besides the increased risk of abscesses and skin damage and the risks associated with injecting any drug, cocaine supplies may often be adulterated with substances that can be harmful if injected.

An overdose is possible, and can cause death from heart or respiratory failure, but this is fairly unusual.

Tobacco
• *Legal status*
It is illegal to sell tobacco products to anyone under the age of 16. Tobacco products may not be advertised on television, and other advertising is restricted by agreements between the tobacco industry and the Government.

- *What is it?*

Tobacco is made from the dried leaves of the tobacco plant. The active ingredient in tobacco is nicotine, a mild stimulant that vaporizes when the tobacco is burned.

- *How is it used?*

Cigarettes are the most commonly used form of tobacco in this country, but it can also be obtained in the form of cigars, made from a stronger tobacco, pipe tobacco, also stronger than cigarette tobacco, and snuff, which is powdered tobacco that can be sniffed up the nose. When tobacco is burned and inhaled, the smoke containing nicotine and other substances is absorbed from the lungs into the bloodstream, rapidly reaching the brain.

- *Effects and symptoms*

The effects of tobacco smoke inhalation are almost immediate, and build up during the smoking of each cigarette, declining rapidly after it is finished. Pulse rate and blood pressure increase, skin temperature is lowered, and appetite is reduced. The smoker feels alert and able to concentrate on the job in hand, even if tired or bored, although someone new to smoking may simply feel dizzy and sick.

- *Dependence potential*

Tolerance to the effects of nicotine builds up rapidly, and dependence is very likely to develop, with most people who begin to smoke becoming regular users. Regular users who stop smoking feel jittery, irritable, depressed, and unable to concentrate, and relapse into continued use is very common. Some users will resort to 'chain smoking' – lighting up a new cigarette as soon as the spent one is extinguished – particularly when performing tasks requiring concentration. It has been said by users who have experienced both that giving up smoking is harder than giving up heroin.

100

- *Dangers*

Smoking is an extremely damaging habit. The risk of heart disease, thrombosis, bronchitis and other chest complaints, strokes, circulatory problems, ulcers, and cancer of the mouth, throat, and lungs all increase with the consumption of tobacco. It is estimated that tobacco contributes to at least 100 000 premature deaths in the UK every year, and that a quarter of young male cigarette smokers will have their deaths hastened by the effects of tobacco use. The smoker is not the only one at risk. Smoking in pregnancy has been shown to increase the risk of miscarriage, low birthweight, and stillbirth, and 'passive smoking' can increase the risk of respiratory problems and asthma in those who inhale the smoke produced by others.

Caffeine

- *Legal status*

The manufacture, sale, distribution, and possession of caffeine are not subject to any legal restrictions, but some tonics containing caffeine are pharmacy-only or prescription-only medicines.

- *What is it?*

Caffeine is a stimulant that occurs naturally in tea and coffee and is added to many soft drinks, painkillers, tonics, and headache remedies.

- *How is it used?*

Caffeine is most commonly, in fact almost universally, taken by mouth in the form of drinks like tea, coffee and cola. Medicines containing caffeine are also taken by mouth, normally in the form of pills.

- *Effects and symptoms*

Like other stimulants, caffeine, in moderate doses, alleviates tiredness and aids concentration, taking effect within an hour and lasting for three to four hours. At higher doses – the amount found in more than five or six cups of instant coffee or tea, fewer of 'real' coffee – coordination is actually impaired, the user may feel anxious, and heart rate and blood pressure may be raised. There can be feelings of anxiety and restlessness. When the effects wear off, there can be a 'rebound' effect of tiredness and lethargy. People consuming the amount of caffeine found in seven or more strong cups of coffee per day can become permanently irritable and anxious, and suffer from headaches and muscular 'twitches'. These effects disappear once they cut down on their caffeine intake.

- *Dependence potential*

Tolerance develops to many of the effects of caffeine, and regular users who consume the equivalent of about six cups of instant coffee per day will suffer withdrawal symptoms, including drowsiness, irritability, and headaches, if they stop suddenly. Many people find that they feel tired and irritable if they can't have their habitual morning cup of tea or coffee. Physical and psychological dependence can develop to the point where it is very hard to give up tea or coffee, even if there are medical reasons for doing so.

- *Dangers*

There is some evidence that heavy and long-term coffee drinking increases the risk of ulcers, heart disease, and even some cancers, but this is inconclusive. People with existing ulcers, high blood pressure, or who suffer from anxiety may find that caffeine aggravates their problem, and caffeine taken late in the day causes insomnia in many people. A fatal overdose is theoretically possible, but would require the amount of caffeine contained in over 100 cups of coffee.

Cannabis
- *Legal status*

A class B, controlled drug in all its readily available forms, but the active ingredients when separated from the plant would be classified as class A.

- *What is it?*

Cannabis is made in a variety of ways from the plant *Cannabis sativa*, which grows wild in many hot, dry countries, but can and has been grown in Britain. It is freely available and relatively cheap, and is probably the most widely used of the illegal drugs. It may be supplied in the form of dried leaves, which are greener in colour than tobacco, and either loose or compressed into blocks or sticks, or as a brown resin compressed into blocks, cakes, or sticks. Rarely in this country, it may also be supplied as an oily extract.

- *How is it used?*

Cannabis is usually combined with tobacco and rolled into a cigarette, but may also be smoked in a pipe or added to food or drink.

- *Effects and symptoms*

The effects of cannabis in average doses are generally very mild, and some people may experience no effects at all from their first uses of the drug. The effects that do occur are usually dependent on the circumstances in which the drug is used and the expectations of the user. In the right setting, perhaps with friends or listening to music, the user will feel relaxed and sociable, and enjoy a deeper appreciation of experiences such as sound, colour and taste. There can also be some feelings of anxiety, particularly in new users who don't know what to expect from the experience. When smoked, the effects of cannabis start after a few minutes and gradually increase. If eaten or drunk, the onset is slower. Someone who is high on cannabis may appear slightly drunk.

Higher doses may cause confusion, forgetfulness, and distortion of the user's sense of time and reality. Occasionally, and particularly in new users or those who were already feeling anxious or depressed, the user may become very distressed and confused. These effects will wear

103

off within a few hours, although they may persist for longer if the drug has been eaten or drunk.

- *Dependence potential*

Cannabis is not thought to produce tolerance or physical dependence. Regular or heavy users may come to rely on the drug as a social aid, rather in the way that many people regard a drink or two as an almost indispensable part of an evening with friends, and so a degree of psychological dependence may arise with heavy use.

- *Dangers*

Smoking cannabis carries a higher risk of respiratory disease, including lung cancer, than does smoking tobacco. Some experiments have suggested the possibility of psychological and physical damage, including permanent brain damage, from long-term use, but the sorts of studies needed to verify these suspicions are necessarily broad in their scope, long-term, and have not yet been carried out. Temporary psychological disturbance can result from heavy use, though, and existing mental conditions may be exaggerated. Most authorities believe that occasional cannabis use is no more dangerous than the moderate use of alcohol or tobacco (see under Alcohol and Tobacco above).

Heavy, regular users who are almost permanently intoxicated may be lethargic and unable to perform as they should at school or work. This level of use does seem to be rare, however. A fatal overdose is virtually impossible. As with any intoxicant, coordination and reaction time may be affected so driving under the influence of cannabis could be dangerous.

Ecstasy (MDMA)
- *Legal status*
A Class A controlled drug.

- *What is it?*

Methylenedioxymethamphetamine is a combined stimulant (amphetamine) and hallucinogenic drug, although at commonly used doses it does not normally produce hallucinations in the way that LSD, for instance, does.

MDMA comes in tablet or capsule form. Various substances have been sold under the guise of ecstasy, including amphetamines, LSD, and even dog worming tablets. Because of the popularity of these drugs, there is a significant danger that 'bathtub' producers will put substandard drugs of dubious purity on to the market, which could result in unpredictable effects on the user.

- *How is it used?*

MDMA is taken exclusively by mouth. It is essentially a social drug, connected with the rave culture, and is widely used by young people to enable them to sustain energetic dancing for long periods without exhaustion.

- *Effects and symptoms*

The effects of MDMA are similar to those of amphetamines, with the addition of a heightening of awareness that users say increases their enjoyment of social contact and the music and light shows associated with the dance culture. The drug begins to take effect between 20 and 60 minutes after taking the pill or capsule. Pupils become dilated, the jaw tightens and there may be a brief feeling of nausea, sweating, dry mouth, a rise in blood pressure and loss of appetite. Coordination can be impaired.

When the drug wears off, the user may experience the same sorts of rebound effects that are associated with amphetamines – tiredness, depression, and aches and pains, which may last for several days.

- *Dependence potential*

MDMA is not physically addictive. It may, however, be difficult for a user to stop using the drug but continue to take part in the social scene in which it is taken, where others will still be using it.

- *Dangers*

There have been a number of deaths in the UK associated with MDMA use. These deaths were apparently related to a rare reaction to the drug, resulting in respiratory failure, although heart failure and brain haemorrhages have also been reported. More common are less serious problems, including fits, headaches, and various unexplained pains. Because of the heightened and extended physical activity often associated with the drug's use, users may suffer from the effects of heat stroke, dehydration, and exhaustion.

Ill effects from the use of MDMA don't seem to depend on dose levels, and it may be that some users are inherently more susceptible to the drug than others or that the circumstances in which they take it heightens the effects of the drug. There doesn't seem to be a 'safe' dose.

There has been some evidence that MDMA use may be associated with liver damage, and it is thought that it may affect the immune system. The increased sexual activity associated with the rave scene may incidentally present a risk of HIV infection.

Some users have reported unpleasant psychological experiences at higher doses, including hallucinations, panic, confusion, and insomnia. These effects usually cease once the effects of the drug wear off, but there may be flashbacks days or even weeks after the event, in which the experience is briefly relived, causing anxiety and confusion.

Because MDMA can affect bodily coordination, users should not drive or operate hazardous machinery while under its influence.

Opiates

- *Legal status*

Heroin, morphine, opium, methadone, dipipanone and pethidine are class A, controlled drugs. Codeine and dihydrocodeine are class B, controlled drugs (but class A if they are prepared for injection). Dextropoxyphene (Distalgesic, etc.) and buprenorphine (Temgesic) are class C, controlled drugs. Very dilute mixtures of codeine, morphine or opium such as some cough or diarrhoea medicines are exempt from most restrictions, and can be bought over the counter in a pharmacy.

It is an offence to use opium, to possess the equipment for smoking opium, to frequent a place used for smoking opium or to allow a place to be used for the preparation or smoking of opium.

- *What are they?*

Opiates are derived from the opium poppy, although there are now synthetic substitutes. They are used legitimately in painkillers, cough suppressants, and diarrhoea medicines. Morphine, for instance, is used medicinally for the relief of pain in cancer sufferers, for whom its addictive potential is not seen as a problem.

- *How are they used?*

Opiates can be taken by mouth, but the effect is greatly enhanced if they are absorbed into the bloodstream by a more direct route, either by sniffing, smoking or injection. Heroin, the most widely used illicit opiate, is most popularly used by heating the powder and inhaling the smoke through a small tube. Hardened users, however, may prefer the more immediate effects of injecting the drug straight into a vein.

Morphine is supplied in powder, tablet, liquid, or ampoules, and is taken by mouth, injected, heated and the vapour inhaled or, occasionally, used as a suppository.

Over-the-counter opiates, such as the codeine contained in cough suppressants, are supplied in the form of a linctus, and are taken by mouth, but these are far less effective and large amounts must be taken. These preparations contain a very small proportion of opiate, and the effects of their other ingredients, when taken in doses high enough to produce the effects sought by opiate users, make them a poor substitute for the more refined, illegal varieties (see Over-the-counter medicines below).

• *Effects and symptoms*

Opiates have a depressant and calming effect on the user. They effectively cushion him from the effects of anxiety, fear and discomfort and reduce the desire for food, sex, and so on, giving the feeling of being 'wrapped in cotton wool'. They will suppress the cough reflex and slow respiration and heart rate, dilate blood vessels, and cause sweating and narrowing of the pupils.

Injection into a vein produces an almost instant and intense reaction, while injection under the skin is slower-acting and less intense, as is sniffing. Smoking heroin means it works quickly, but the effect is less intense than injecting.

• *Dependence potential*

Opiates are highly addictive. Tolerance and physical dependence develop quickly with repeated use, so that the user must take higher and higher doses and adopt more direct routes of administration to achieve the same effect. The user who has an established opiate habit will experience unpleasant withdrawal symptoms, including sweating, anxiety, muscle cramps, fever, and diarrhoea if she ceases to take the drug, and the reaction can be severe enough to be fatal in a very heavy regular user. After a while, the heavy user will cease to experience the pleasurable effects of the drug, but will need to take it regularly just to avoid the unpleasantness of withdrawal and to feel 'normal'.

• *Dangers*

Opiates do little direct harm to the body in moderate doses, even with long-term use, although a fatal overdose is possible, especially where a regular user has stopped using for a time and so lost some physical tolerance, then resumes use at the dose he was using before the break. Illegal drugs are always an unknown quantity, and it is not uncommon for street heroin to be adulterated with substances that can cause fatal reactions if injected, or for them to be unexpectedly pure and lead to an accidental overdose. Taking other depressant drugs at the same time as opiates can also lead to unpredictably heightened and possibly dangerous effects.

The major danger to opiate users arises from the lifestyle that goes with regular drug use, and from the dangers associated with injecting drugs. People who use opiates regularly may become apathetic and neglect themselves, risking health problems arising from poor nutrition, lack of hygiene, and poor living conditions. The need to ensure a daily supply of drugs in order to avoid withdrawal may lead to serious financial problems, and the user may resort to crime, prostitution, or some other risky means to finance the habit. Regular heroin sniffing can cause damage to the nose.

Hallucinogens

LSD (Lysergic acid diethylamide)
- *Legal status*

A class A controlled drug.

- *What is it?*

LSD is derived from a fungus (ergot) which grows on rye and other plants. It was originally developed for use in psychotherapy, but, following an explosion in its non-medical use by hippie and other groups, it was placed under the Misuse of Drugs Act in the 1960s and quickly fell out of medical use.

In its pure form, LSD is a white powder, but as only tiny amounts are used for a trip, it is normally supplied as an impregnated square of paper or gelatine, often printed with cartoon characters or colourful patterns, or made into tablets (usually very small) or capsules. Much of what is sold on the street as LSD may actually contain little or no LSD at all, and its strength, at the best of times, is uncertain. The use of LSD has undergone an upsurge among people in the 15-24 age bracket since the advent of the rave scene, where it may be used along with amphetamines and ecstasy to enhance the experience of music and light shows.

- *How is it used?*

LSD is taken exclusively by mouth, taking effect after about 30 minutes, intensifying over 2 to 6 hours, and fading after about 12 hours, depending on the dose taken. One impregnated square of paper or tablet represents a normal dose, although more may be taken.

- *Effects and symptoms*

A moderate dose of LSD will produce intensification and distortion of sensory experiences, such as colour, sound, and touch. The user may 'see' sounds and 'hear' colours, her surroundings may seem to shift and change, and her sense of time may be distorted. Usually, the user is aware that these distortions are not real.

The user may have feelings of heightened self-awareness and mystical knowledge, although what he feels at the time to be the discovery of a great truth may turn out later to be a meaningless phrase or banality. While many trips are harmless or pleasant, some may be frightening and depressing, particularly if the user was feeling anxious or unhappy before taking the drug. Sometimes the same trip may combine pleasant and terrifying elements, and occasionally, at higher doses, full-blown hallucinations may occur, in which the user loses contact completely with reality and believes himself to be in some threatening or dangerous situation.

- *Dependence potential*

Physical dependence does not occur with LSD use. Tolerance builds up very rapidly, to the point where the drug becomes ineffective after a few days' use, and the user has to stop for at least three or four days before using again. Psychological dependence is very rare.

- *Dangers*

LSD acts mainly on the mind, with very little physical effect, even from long-term use. It would, however, be very difficult to undertake any task requiring concentration while tripping on LSD, and driving would be very unwise. Unpleasant psychological effects are possible at any dose, but more common in regular users. It is possible, though rare, that a user might injure herself or others while gripped by a hallucination – there have been a few well-publicized incidents of people throwing themselves off buildings while under the influence of LSD, believing that they could fly, or attacking others believing that they are themselves being threatened or attacked. Some users have remained psychologically disturbed after a bad trip long after the drug itself has worn off although, again, this is rare, and some experience flashbacks, that is, re-experiences of an earlier trip that occur unexpectedly even though no further LSD has been taken.

Hallucinogenic (magic) mushrooms
- *Legal status*

Psilocin- or psilocybin-containing mushrooms in their freshly picked state are not restricted by law, but preparing them in any way (even drying or crushing), or growing, or possessing them with intent to supply is illegal, as both substances are class A, controlled drugs.

- *What are they?*

There are several varieties of hallucinogenic mushroom growing wild in Britain. Most commonly used are the Fly Agaric (*Amanita muscaria),* which does not contain psilocin or psilocybin, and the Liberty Cap (*Psilocybe semilanceata*), which does. They can be picked fresh in early autumn, and may be dried for later use.

- *How are they used?*

The whole mushroom is picked and eaten raw or cooked, or brewed into a tea. Dried mushrooms are taken in the same way. As many as 20 or 30 mushrooms may be required for a hallucinogenic experience similar to a mild dose of LSD, although their potency is very variable and affected by the method of preparation.

- *Effects and symptoms*

The effects of these mushrooms are the same as those resulting from a mild dose of LSD, with the addition of dilated pupils, increased heart rate and blood pressure, and other physical symptoms. The effects start within about half an hour, and reach their height within around three hours, depending on the dose, and last about four to nine hours. The user will often suffer stomach pain and vomiting.

- *Dependence potential*

As for LSD.

- *Dangers*

The greatest danger is that of eating one of the highly toxic varieties of fungi that grow wild in Britain, mistaking them for hallucinogenic mushrooms. While the Fly Agaric and Liberty Cap could cause a fatal overdose only if taken in enormous quantities, some species can kill if eaten in very small amounts.

As with LSD, bad trips and psychological disturbance are a possibility, but reassurance and support will usually get the user through the experience, and the effects rarely last beyond the end of the trip. Flashbacks can occur, but usually fade with time.

Other drugs

Amyl and butyl nitrite
- *Legal status*

Amyl nitrite is classified as a pharmacy medicine, but is hardly ever stocked by pharmacists. Butyl nitrite is not classified as a drug, and there are no restrictions on its availability.

- *What are they?*

Amyl and butyl nitrite (collectively known as alkyl nitrites) are clear, yellow, volatile liquids. Amyl nitrite has been used in the treatment of angina and as an antidote to cyanide poisoning. Butyl nitrite has no medical uses. They are supplied in small glass bottles with screw or plug tops or, occasionally, in small glass capsules wrapped in cotton wool.

- *How are they taken?*

Both substances are inhaled, either straight from the bottle or from a cloth.

- *Effects and symptoms*

Alkyl nitrites dilate the blood vessels and relax muscles. Their muscle-relaxant properties appealed first to the male gay community, who used them to facilitate homosexual intercourse, but the rush experienced as the blood vessels dilate and heartbeat quickens, sending a rush of blood to the brain, also appeals to a wider range of users, and the drug is becoming more widely used. These effects last only for a few minutes, resulting in dizziness, facial flushing, and headache.

- *Dependence potential*

Tolerance develops after two or three weeks of continual use, but abates after a few days without use. Neither physical nor psychological dependence or withdrawal symptoms seem to be a problem.

- *Dangers*

Sniffing of nitrites has occasionally been reported to cause dermatitis of the upper lip, nose and cheeks, and pain and swelling of the nasal passages. These symptoms clear up if sniffing is discontinued. Very heavy use may result in a reduction of oxygen in the blood, which can cause vomiting, shock, and unconsciousness. This condition can lead to death, although those cases that have been reported have usually been of people who have swallowed the substance

113

rather than inhaled it. The danger of serious consequences of this sort is greater for anyone with heart trouble or anaemia. Because the drug leaves the body rapidly after use, there don't seem to be any serious long-term problems arising from the inhalation of nitrites by healthy individuals.

Anabolic steroids
* *Legal status*

Prescription-only drugs that can only be sold by a pharmacist on production of a doctor's prescription. As they are not yet controlled under the Misuse of Drugs Act, possession for personal use is not illegal, although new controls are under consideration.

* *What are they?*

Anabolic steroids are a group of hormones that occur naturally in the body, and control the development and functioning of the reproductive organs. Testosterone, the most important of the male steroidal hormones, and the one from which most of the synthetic anabolic steroids on the market are derived, is also responsible for the development of male characteristics, such as deepened voice and the growth of body hair. Anabolic steroids also have the effect of building up muscle, and it is this effect that has led to their medical use in the treatment of anaemia, thrombosis, and muscle wasting and to their illicit use among bodybuilders.

* *How are they used?*

Anabolic steroids are supplied in the form of tablets or as an injectable solution, usually available from contacts at the user's gymnasium or sports club. Bodybuilders and athletes generally use them during training over a six- to eight-week cycle, and in doses far higher than would be recommended for medical use.

* *Effects and symptoms*

Steroids make the user feel more aggressive, and enable him to train harder. They can help to increase muscle bulk and strength, which is the effect usually sought by bodybuilders.

- *Dependence potential*

Physical dependence does not seem to be a problem, although psychological dependence can occur. Some users say that they feel depressed and lethargic when they stop taking the drug, and athletes who believe that the drug enhances their performance may not be able to face giving up their advantage.

- *Dangers*

Long-term use is believed to lead to liver and kidney damage and tumours, increased blood pressure, impaired growth in young people, and to temporary psychiatric disorders. In men, repeated use may lead to sterility and impotence, while women may develop menstrual irregularities, and masculine characteristics such as deepened voice, facial and body hair, and decreased breast size. These changes cannot be reversed. Steroids taken during pregnancy can seriously damage the baby.

The increase in aggression caused by steroids, sometimes referred to as 'roid rage' or 'steroid mania' has been blamed for violent crimes, particularly incidents of domestic violence and child abuse, and used as a defence in court in some cases.

Where steroids are injected, the usual risks involved with injecting apply, as do the risks of impurity and uncertain strength connected with any illicit drug. Some of the anabolic steroids available illicitly were manufactured for use on animals rather than people, while others are counterfeits of legitimate brands.

Over-the-counter drugs

Many drugs with abuse potential are available without prescription, either from registered pharmacies under the supervision of a pharmacist or in unregistered shops. Antihistamines may be used for their sedative effect or mixed with heroin or methadone. The amphetamine-like substances in decongestants may be used as a stimulant, and painkillers, cough linctuses, and diarrhoea treatments may be taken in large doses for their opiate content. These practices can be highly dangerous because, in order to obtain the desired effect from the element of the preparation in which the user is interested, it is necessary for him to take very large doses of its other ingredients. Some of these, such as the paracetamol often combined with codeine in painkillers, can be very damaging indeed.

If you find a drug you can't identify and are worried that your child may be misusing it, your best course of action is to ask her what it is, although you could try to get it identified before you tackle her (see Chapter 5; for quick reference see the check-list showing each drug's proprietary and street names, and the tell-tale signs of use associated with it, on pages 117-122; for further information on tolerance, dependence, and addiction, see Chapter 2).

Check-list of Drugs - Their Names, Effects, and Signs of Use.

Substance	Proprietary names	Street names	Effects	Signs of use
Benzodiazepines	Valium Temazepam Librium Ativan	Tranx, tems, eggs, jellies.	Sedation, slurred speech, euphoria, disorientation, drunken behaviour.	Tablets or capsules, which may be crushed or opened for injection. Syringes and needles, injection marks.
Barbiturates	Tuinal Seconal Amytal	Barbs, candy, goofballs, sleeping pills, peanuts, downers, sleepers, reds and blues, rainbows, double troubles, red birds, red devils, reds, seggy, angels, birds, blue heavens.		
Amphetamines and amphetamine-like drugs	Dexedrine, Ritalin, Apisate, Tenuate, Duromine, Ionamin, Volital.	'A', uppers, pep pills, diet pills, jelly beans, truck drivers, co-pilots, eye-openers, wake-ups, dexies, rities, meth, speed, crystal, crank, ice, glass.	Raised blood pressure, breathing and heart rate, dilated pupils, flushed appearance, talkativeness, reduced appetite, possibly aggression.	Folded wraps of paper about 2 x 2 in. when unfolded, white, greyish white, pink, or yellow powder, tablets, needles and syringes.

Substance	Proprietary names	Street names	Effects	Signs of use
Solvents: Acetate, benzene, carbon tetrachloride, chloroform, cyclotexane, ethyl ether, acetone, mexane, naptha, perchlorethylene, toluene, trichlorethylene, trichlorophane, various alcohols.	Found in many brands of aerosol spray (as propellants), lighter fluid, solvent-based glues, dry-cleaning fluids, chemical solvents, butane gas (found in cigarette lighters and refills and used in many aerosols), paint stripper, etc., petrol, dyes, nail polish and remover, rubber solutions, typewriter correction fluid and thinner.		Stomach cramps, uncoordinated movements and slurred speech, drunken behaviour, inflamed eyes.	Rash around nose and mouth, empty tubes or cans, plastic bags with traces of glue in them, strong chemical smell, traces of substances on clothing.
Cannabis	Not misused in a proprietary form.	Cannabis, marijuana, hash, THC, pot, grass, wacky, baccy, hash, Ganja, oil, dope.	Impaired coordination, slightly drunken appearance. At higher doses, confusion, forgetfulness, occasionally anxiety and distress.	Butt ends of hand-rolled cigarettes (joints), large cigarette papers, strong herbal-type smell of burning leaves.

Substance	Proprietary names	Street names	Effects	Signs of use
Cocaine, freebase, and crack	Not misused in a proprietary form.	Coke, snow, sleigh ride, white lady.	Increased pulse rate and blood pressure, dilated and light-sensitive pupils, sleeplessness, talkativeness, possibly aggression, anxiety and hallucinations at high doses, lethargy and depression as drug wears off.	Folded wraps of paper, mirror and razor blade, straw for sniffing/snorting, rolled up bank notes, needles and syringes, small plastic bags, pipes, rocks of cocaine.
Ecstasy (MDMA)	Not misused in a proprietary form.	Adam, XTC, fantasy, big brown ones, burgers, california sunrise, disco biscuits, love doves, new yorkers, M25s, pink skuds, Dennis the Menace.	Increased energy, sleeplessness. Thirst, depression, and tiredness as drug wears off.	Tablets or capsules.

Substance	Proprietary names	Street names	Effects	Signs of use
Heroin	Not misused in a proprietary form.	H, horse, scag, smack, stuff, scat, Chinese 'H', tiger, chi, harry, junk, elephant, dragon.	Drowsiness, narrowed pupils, sweating, reduced respiration and heart rate, nausea.	Wraps of paper, syringes and needles, blackened tin foil, tourniquet (belt, tie, or string), bent spoons, spent matches, bottle caps, needle marks on hands, arms, legs, or feet, blood stains on clothing and bedding.
Other opiates and opioids (synthetic opiates): opium, morphine, methadone, pethidine, dipipanone, codeine, etc.	Sevredol, MST Continus, Cyclimorph, Omnopon, Scopolomine, Nepenthe, Temgesic, DF118, Diconal, Physeptone, Palfium, and several proprietary cough suppressants, painkillers, and antidiarrhoea medicines contain relatively small amounts of opiates.	Dike, amps, linctus.	As for heroin.	Tablets, ampoules, linctus, suppositories, injecting equipment.

Substance	Proprietary names	Street names	Effects	Signs of use
LSD (Lysergic acid diethylamide)	Not misused in a proprietary form.	Acid, blotters, tabs.	Few physical effects, but heightened awareness, distortion of sensory perception, sometimes hallucinations and panic.	Small tablets or squares of paper.
Hallucinogenic mushrooms	Not misused in a proprietary form.	Magic mushrooms.	As for LSD, but often with stomach pains, nausea, and vomiting.	Fresh or dried mushrooms, tablets made from mushrooms, looking and smelling similar to yeast tablets.
Amyl and butyl nitrite	Rush, Quick Silver, Liquid Gold, Bolt, etc.	Nitrates, poppers, bananas, snappers, rush.	Flushing, quickened heartbeat, dizziness, headache.	Small glass bottles with screw or plug tops, glass capsules wrapped in cotton wool.

Substance	Proprietary names	Street names	Effects	Signs of use
Anabolic steroids	Too many to list in entirety, but including Atamestane, Bolazine, Bolmantalate, Durabolin, Dianabol, Methenolone, Mibolerone, Nandrolone, Ovandrotone, Epitiostanol, Fluoxymesterone, Oxymesterone, Stanozolol, Silandrone, Triolostane.		Increased aggression and energy in training.	Pills, capsules or bottles of injectable solution and injecting equipment.

Useful addresses

Standing Conference on Drug Abuse (SCODA)
1/4 Hatton Place
Hatton Garden
London EC1N 8ND
Telephone: 0171-430 2341
Coordinates the activities of independent voluntary drug
agencies. Produces a directory of drug services entitled
'Drug Problems:where to get help'. Also runs a freephone
helpline – just dial 100 and ask for 'freephone drug
problems'.

Institute for the Study of Drug Dependence (ISDD)
Waterbridge House
32-36 Loman Street
London SE1 0EE
Telephone: 0171-928 1211
Provides information on drugs and drug misuse. Send a large
stamped and self-addressed envelope to receive their
extensive publications list.

ADFAM National
82 Old Brompton Road
London SW7 3LQ
Telephone: 0171-823 9313
National helpline, information, advice and counselling for the
families and friends of drug users. ADFAM also provides
training and project support for professionals and volunteers
working with the families of drug users.

Re-Solv (The Society for the Prevention of Solvent and
Volatile Substance Abuse)
30a High Street
Stone
Staffordshire ST15 8AW
Telephone: 01785 817885
Has information on solvent abuse and a directory of
agencies that can help.

Solvent Misuse Project
National Children's Bureau
8 Wakley Street
London EC1V 7QE
Telephone: 0171-278 9441
Produces a directory of residential services that accept young
solvent abusers.

Release
388 Old Street
London EC1V 9LT
Telephone: 0171-729 9904
24-hour legal emergency helpline: 071-603 8654
For drug information and advice.

Youth Access
Magazine Business Centre
11 Newarke Street
Leicester LE1 5SS
Telephone: 01162 558763
A young people's counselling agency that will be able to put
you in touch with counsellors in your area.

Exploring Parenthood
Latimer Education Centre
194 Freston Road
London W10 6TT
Telephone: 0181-960 1678
Information and workshops for parents exploring the issues
of parenthood. Send a stamped, self-addressed envelope for
a publications list.

Positive Prevention Plus
3 Radnor Way
Slough
Berkshire SL3 7LA
Telephone: 01753 542296
A charitable trust providing support and training for parents
in parenting skills for drug abuse prevention.

Familes Anonymous
The Doddington and Rollo Community Association
Charlotte Despard Avenue
Battersea London SW11 5JE
Telephone: 0171-498 4680
A self-help group for relatives and friends concerned about
the use of drugs or related behavioural problems. Write,
enclosing stamped, self-addressed envelope, or ring for
details of local groups.

Parent Network
44-46 Caversham Road
Kentish Town
London NW5 2DS
Telephone: 0171-485 8535
A national network of local parent support groups, helping
parents and children to feel better about themselves and each
other, and handle the ups and downs of family life.

Parents Anonymous
Telephone: 0171-263 8918
Advice and help for parents having problems with their children.

Parentline
Telephone: 01268 757077
A network of parent-run groups offering telephone listening and support to parents under stress. Will often be able to provide details of other local sources of help. Ring this number for details of your local group.

Narcotics Anonymous
UK Service Office
PO Box 1980
London N19 3LS
Helpline: 0171-351 6794
Recorded meeting list: 0171-351 6066
Publications: 0171-272 9040
Self-help group for drug users.

Further reading

Drugs and drug problems

Drugs and your child. Institute for the study of Drug Dependence 1992.
This booklet contains practical advice and support for parents worried about drug abuse.

Goodsir, Jane, *Drugs and the Law*. Release Publications Ltd 1991.
A booklet that is a useful guide to the Misuse of Drugs Act 1971 with advice on the rights of those arrested for drugs offences.

The Royal College of Psychiatrists, *Drug Scenes*. Gaskell 1987.
A report on drugs and drug dependence by the Royal College of Psychiatrists. An interesting and readable insight into a complex subject.

Standing Conference on Drug Abuse, *Drug Problems: Where to get help*. SCODA 1992.
National directory of drug services in England, the Isle of Wight, Wales, and the Channel Islands, plus information on national services for Scotland and a contact point for help in Northern Ireland.

Stockley, David, *Drug Warning: An illustrated guide for parents, teachers and employers*. Optima 1992.
A detailed guide to commonly and less commonly misused drugs, heavily illustrated with colour photographs, which makes the identification of substances possible in many cases.

All these are available from the Institute for the Study of Drug Dependence (see page 123 for the address), which also produces a series of leaflets on individual drugs, provides information on drug problems, and keeps an extensive reference and research library.

Family life

Baker, Carol, *Getting on with Your Children*. Longman 1990.

Crabtree, Tom, *A-Z of Children's Emotional Problems*. Unwin 1984.

Jacques, Penny, *Understanding Children's Problems*. Unwin 1987.

All these books provide readable and practical insights into understanding and coping with the ups and downs of family life. Also see other books in the Sheldon Press Overcoming Common Problems series for practical help with family problems, such as *Helping Children Cope with Stress, Helping Children Cope with Grief, Helping Children Cope with Divorce, How to Survive Your Teenagers,* and others.

Index

accidents 12

addiction and dependence: children susceptible to drugs 13-15; difference between addiction and dependence 15-16; treatment and rehabilitation 64-8, 72

ADFAM National 58

adulteration 12-13

adults: use statistics 3

alcohol 2, 87, 91-2; depressant effect 10; effect on children 8; justifying to children 24-5, 27; supply 85

amphetamines 10, 95-7, 117; dance culture 6; laws 78; price 7; use statistics 4

amyl nitrite 12, 112-14, 121

anabolic steroids 11, 114-15, 122

antihistamines 11, 115

Balding, John 4

barbiturates 89-90, 117 *see* depressants; laws 77

benzodiazepines 87-9, 117; laws 78, 79

butyl nitrite 12, 79, 112-14, 121

caffeine 101-2

cannabinol: laws 77

cannabis 11, 102-4, 118; growing 81; illegality 24-5; laws 77, 78, 84; price 7; use statistics 3-4

child guidance clinics 55, 56

children: age and the law 82-3; allowing independence 34; confidence 17, 33-4; creating the right environment 34-7; detecting use of drugs 38-41; developing ways of coping 28-9; effects of drug taking 7-9; responsibility for decisions 25; statistics of drug use 4; talking to about drugs 17-26, 43; where they might encounter drugs 6-7; who is likely to take drugs 13-15; who might try drugs 5-6

Citizens' Advice Bureaux 58

cocaine 10, 98-9, 119; encountering 6; laws 77, 78; price 7; use statistics 4